PSYCHIC DIMENSIONS

My Investigations at the Isabella Stewart Gardner Museum

Predicting the Pope Would Be Shot

Finding Lost Valuables

Speaking and Writing in Other Languages

Spirit Contact

Time Travel

UFOs

Donna DiPietro

CONTENTS

CHAPTER 1: The Beginning
  Angelic Beings
  The Ball
  Spirit Light
  Voice in the Hallway

CHAPTER 2: House of Time Travel

CHAPTER 3: My Investigations at the Isabella Stewart Gardner Museum

CHAPTER 4: Finding Lost Valuables
  Diamond and Sapphire Rings
  Gold Bracelet
  Mother's Bracelet
  Heart-Shaped Pendant
  The Attic Room
  Valuable Photos
  Tiffany Necklace
  Moving Day
  Kodak Medallion
  Psychic GPS

CHAPTER 5: Predicting the Future
  The Pope was Shot
  World of Music
  Dear Mindy
  Nimble Thimble

Future Son and Daughter
Twin Boys
The Race Horse Gentleman

CHAPTER 6: Making Contact
I Spoke in German and Wrote in Polish
Paranormal Activity - Gilmanton Iron Works
Haunted House - Belfast, Maine
Guiding a Spirit to the Light
Dead Man in Garage
Ghost Dog
Bridget Bishop – Salem Witch Trials

CHAPTER 7: Unusual Events
Maps of the Brain
Syracuse University – Book of Names
The Bank Vault
Church of Spirits
Potting Soil
Missing Girl Found
Swedish Fish

CHAPTER 8: A Glimpse of Heaven - My Near Death Experience

CHAPTER 9: Contact with Al

CHAPTER 10: Meeting Betty Hill - UFO Case 'The Interrupted Journey'

SCIENTIFIC PROSPECTIVE

It has not been determined how exactly psychic abilities work but some scientists have come up with a possible answer. We are spiritual beings and spirit is a form of energy which comprises waves, created by vibration of subatomic particles – electrons. This allows the spirit to travel to places, as an energy, to interact with other energetic beings: human and non-human. This energetic interaction leads to observation and/or information exchange. Therefore, chosen people, with developed psychic abilities, are capable of traveling to places that they have never been before, to find lost or stolen items, or to speak/read in different languages that they have never learned. The energy of spirit travels very fast and, in many cases, by the psychic's intentional focus on a subject.
PS: reference to Albert Tsagikyan, PhD.

INTRODUCTION

Dear Readers:

I hope that you enjoy my stories as much as I enjoy sharing them with you. When we reach a certain age, we often realize that it is important to document special events in our lives or the details will be lost forever. It is only within the last few years that I have received answers to some important questions regarding the paranormal. Many people are afraid of spirits and anything related to them. Perhaps this has something to do with the abundance of television programs and movies that often portray spirits as malevolent and frightful beings. In reality, a spirit is a person who has passed over because his or her body is no longer a suitable means of transport. All of us will pass over sometime and we will be the same as them. They were once living their lives and doing many of the same things that we do. If you have lost a loved one, would you not want to see that person again and have them visit you? They love you and would never want to frighten or harm you.

The paranormal is a part of who we are. We call it para'normal since we cannot explain it in the normal sense. Events, such as these, have happened throughout history. They are inspirational in religious beliefs and give hope and comfort to those who believe. They may not be able to explain them but they have great faith that these events have occurred.

In relation to my own psychic experiences, I have discovered that there are other dimensions around us and, for some reason, I am able to traverse these dimensions to see places, to find things, to visit the past, to predict the future and to make contact with people who are living and those who have passed. Sometimes, I can see a person or groups of people that I do not know but they seem unable to see me, as though we are from different dimensions. Perhaps, that is the same experience we have when people, who have passed, visit us, and we do not see them. Often, a person who is getting ready to pass will see loved ones who have passed. They may also see people that they do not know. Those who are passing describe these people as kind and comforting. Some are dressed in clothing reminiscent of many years ago and have hair styles of that same time period. There are logical explanations for some of these visions, but not all, where the person, who is getting ready to pass, may be having hallucinations caused by their condition and/or medications.

Some of my cases are experiences that I have had in communicating with those who have passed over. Mediumship communication is very different than telepathy when I read someone's thoughts or memories. When I experience mediumship and make contact with a spirit, I see the deceased person, as they looked in life, and feel his or her presence and strong emotions. They will often use me to get their message across to a loved one. For a spirit to do this, it comes into my dimension to make contact. When the communication is over, I feel a sense of calmness in my surroundings and I know that the spirit has gone. It is a different experience when I predict the future and when I find lost valuables, as these require that I go into other dimensions.

When I use my gift for mediumship, time traveling to dimensions and paranormal investigations, I am in a relaxed state of mind connecting with spirit. It is a very pleasant natural feeling that I describe as 'one step up' from Earth. Telepathy is different and I am in direct contact even if that person is thousands of miles away. Precognition can be both good and bad, depending on what I envision.

I have to try to figure out my own psychic experiences for myself. I am blessed to not only have psychic abilities and a logical mind but I am a researcher who seeks the truth. I want to share with the readers how it feels to have a special gift that I did not understand, and at times, did not believe, until it was proven to me, one step at a time. My parents were always accepting of my gift and they and others, from past generations, shared some of it themselves. Back then, people did not talk about such things, except on rare occasions, so most of those stories have been lost forever. I am fortunate that, today, people are more open to psychic phenomena and they would like to learn about it. Some of the readers may have had their own experiences and want to compare notes.

I have come to the conclusion that psychic abilities are not as unusual as society suggests. The more we learn, the more we understand and those are good steps toward the advancement of the human race.

As a child, I was sometimes frightened of things that happened to me without a logical explanation. But when family members experienced some of these events with me, it was proof that they were real. Though it was fascinating and mysterious, there was also something very good about it – the fact that I was able to connect to loving beings and dimensions of time.

As a teenager, I did not bother with my abilities and put them aside, so as not to appear different. But once I hit my twenties, my gift presented itself in the most wonderful ways. I finally accepted it and it has been both entertaining and helpful to others since. Though, at times, during my years as a working parent of young children, I did put it aside until I was contacted for assistance.

My psychic gift comes with a great responsibility. There are some things that I am not supposed to know and there are instances when I cannot make a connection. In the last few years, I have realized how important that my gift is and how it has, not only changed my life, but has helped to change other people's lives. Each case has advanced my knowledge of the paranormal and I am ever so grateful to God for such a wonderful gift. I do not consider myself a professional psychic since I have never charged or accepted payment for helping people. I feel that my mission on Earth is to use good positive energy that connects to others and they, in turn, help to multiply this energy throughout the world and that is what this world needs.

CHAPTER 1

THE BEGINNING

ANGELIC BEINGS

In the beginning, the angelic beings first appeared to me when I was about three years old. They showed themselves as cherubic heads and shoulders and gathered around the living room ceiling watching over me. Loving and protective, I sensed that they were related to me in some way. Though it felt natural and comforting, I did not understand who they were and why I was able to see them. For many years after, I was not sure if this was influenced by my childhood imagination or if it was something real. It is only within the last few years that they have once again appeared and have given me proof of their existence. They now appear as full body angelic beings and they are indeed loving and protective and guide me on my life's journey.

THE BALL

As a child, I wished I had my own dog to play with and love. I was the youngest of six children, living in an apartment, so there was no room for a dog. Nonetheless, I wanted a dog so badly, that I pretended that my dodge ball was a dog and I would call it to come to me and a few times it did. On one occasion, when I was about seven years old, I was alone and standing in the back yard at the bottom of the stairs. The ball was in a corner on the first floor porch where I had placed it the day before. I looked at the ball and concentrated on it to come to me as a dog would when called. After a few minutes, the ball started to move and slowly travelled across the porch to the top of the stairs. It then slowly bounced down the steps, one at a time, until it stopped at my feet. I was surprised and tried to figure out how this could possibly happen.

On another occasion, a friend was over and we were playing catch with the ball when it got caught in a large bush that was against the house and near to where the ball bounced down the steps. My friend went to the bush to get the ball but could not reach it because it was lodged in the branches too far back. I then went to the bush and also tried and failed to reach the ball. As we stood in front of the bush, without touching it, the ball started to slowly move, dislodged itself from the thick branches and came toward me until I held it in my hands. My friend looked at me and asked how I did that and I said I did not know. At that point, I was a little frightened and thought I had better not try to move the ball again.

In the ensuing years, I have tried to come up with an explanation of how the ball could have moved without someone or something touching it. I could not imagine that I would actually be able to make the ball move by using my mind since I did not learn about telekinesis until many years later. It is a bit unsettling because if I was able to move the ball with my thoughts, how do I know I would have control in stopping it from moving?

SPIRIT LIGHT

The light made its first known appearance when I was eight years old and living on Porter Street. One day, my brother, Doug, noticed that there was a light following me. He pointed it out on the dining room wall and that is when my father, my sister, Bess, and I saw it for the first time. It was about the size of a quarter and white. At first, I thought my brother was playing a joke on me but that was not the case. We ruled out a reflection of any kind when my father placed his hand over the light on the wall and there was no reflection on his hand. As the days went by, I was afraid that the light would appear and it did, right before my eyes, and oftentimes when I was alone. It was stationary at first and then moved slowly around the room as though examining it. It followed me for five days then disappeared. One day, my mother and I were home by ourselves. She was in the kitchen sitting on a chair with her back toward me while putting white lace curtains on a stretch rack to dry. I was standing at the threshold from the hallway to the kitchen and I saw the light appear on the narrow wall between the hallway and pantry. I called to my mother to look at the light, as she had not yet seen it. Before she could turn around, the light went inside the pantry as if to hide. I stood in the doorway and watched it travel and I followed it as my apprehension gave way to wonder. I stood still against the pantry counter and watched it go along and stop to examine each object on the shelves in front of me. It seemed to find what it wanted when it came to a large red bowl to hide behind. It went around to the back of the bowl where it stayed on the wall for about five seconds and then disappeared. At this point, I sensed its good energy emitting toward me and I, in turn, felt a protective kinship with a loving being.

  The light was not seen again until about two years later when my mother, father, sister Bess, two brothers and I were visiting my Aunt Sarah Krug in Lakeport, New Hampshire. One night, while my father and two brothers were sleeping in a third floor attic bedroom, my father awoke and saw an exact light on the wall above my brothers' bed. The light was stationary for a while then traveled slowly around the room as though examining it, just as the previous light had done. Eventually, my father got out of bed and went over to the light. He placed his hand over it and there was no reflection on his hand. There were no outside lights, no inside lights, no cars. The room was in total darkness except for the mysterious light. He watched the light for at least a half hour before it disappeared. As before, the light showed intelligence and curiosity. It has been many years since the light made an appearance but perhaps this entity continues to visit but no longer appears as a small white light. An eight-year-old child has an imagination but when witnesses, including a parent and older siblings, share a paranormal event, it sparks a lifetime of searching for answers.

VOICE IN THE HALLWAY

This strange event happened in our Porter Street home when I was in elementary school. At the time, my mother was a stay-at-home mom and would always be there when my brother Doug and I arrived home after school. One day, our mother told us that she was going to Boston to do some shopping and should be home when we got out of school but there was a chance she would be late and, if so, we were to wait inside the front hall. When my brother and I arrived home that day, we walked up to our second floor apartment and knocked on the door but there was no answer. Since our mother was not yet home, we sat on the hall stairs to await her return. The stairs were always clean since my parents washed them each week. The bannisters and woodwork were dark wood and polished but, being an old house, there was a certain smell of age, an atmosphere of silence and a sense of not being alone. As Doug and I sat on the second floor landing, we both heard a woman's voice call out "Douglas". It was a sweet voice and sounded exactly like our mother. Again, the voice called his name. We were both frightened and ran down the stairs and out the front door. We did not even want to sit on the outside steps so we stood on the sidewalk, hoping to see our mother coming up the street. About ten minutes later, we saw her from a distance as she walked up Porter Street from the bus stop. We ran to greet her and, at that moment, she was the most welcome sight imaginable.

CHAPTER 2

HOUSE OF TIME TRAVEL

In Chapter Two, I have documented the paranormal events that occurred at the Cherry Street residence during the thirty years that my parents lived there. While doing research on the house, I found that there is a connection with the family who lived there in the 1870s and Isabella Stewart Gardner whose Boston museum was robbed of valuable art work in 1990 and is known as the 'The World's Greatest Art Heist'; and I, in some strange way, was contacted to help on the case in 2008. In another unusual twist, the man who lived in the house, in the 1870s, was Daniel Damon (sometimes spelled 'Demmon') and I learned that actor Matt Damon lived in the house five years after my parents moved out. Daniel Damon and Matt Damon were both from the neighboring city of Cambridge. Through further research, I found that after Daniel became very wealthy in banking, real estate and copper mining, he sold the Cherry Street house and moved to Beacon Street in Boston at the time that Isabella Stewart Gardner and her husband, Jack, resided in the same neighborhood on Beacon Street. Jack Gardner was also into banking, real estate and copper mining. The Gardners loved to entertain and would often have friends over for dinner, so it is logical that they socialized with Daniel Damon. I also learned that one of Daniel's two daughters married a man with the last name 'Gardner', though I do not know if he was related to Mrs. Gardner's husband.

You will find the documentation of my psychic investigations at the Isabella Stewart Gardner Museum in Chapter Three.

In 1956, my family moved to the top floor apartment of a three-family home on Cherry Street in Somerville, Massachusetts. Built in the 1870s, it was a spacious, square-shaped, red brick mansion set upon a hill. Being the highest house around, we could see for miles over the rooftops of buildings and had great views of Boston, Cambridge and the surrounding area. Each level had seventeen steps to the next floor and, since the house was built on a retaining wall, it had another thirteen steps to reach the first floor. We had to climb forty-seven steps to reach our third floor apartment. There were old gaslights, that no longer worked, hanging on the walls of the inside staircase. Each of the three apartments had seven large rooms with high ceilings. Our reception room had a beautiful working gas fireplace that was surrounded by green marble tiles etched with the faces of ancient Romans. Above the fireplace was a mantle where we hung our Christmas stockings. An old upright piano sat against a wall in the living room. There were large porches on one side and on the front of the house on all three floors. Our floor, being on the top level, did not have roofs on the porches, which gave us the benefit of enjoying sunny summer days and a clear view of the starry night sky. The house was very intriguing and I loved it the moment that I stepped inside. I was the youngest of six children and my two eldest sisters, Elsie and Mae, were married and did not live with us. Six of us resided in the Cherry Street house: my parents, my sister Bess, my two brothers, Robert and Douglas, and me. I still remember the aroma of Pine-Sol as my parents cleaned the apartment in preparation for our moving in. My eldest sister, Elsie, lived with her husband and their three children directly across the street.

CHARLOTTE MAKES HERSELF KNOWN

Our house had some unusual characteristics. Every so often, when we were in the kitchen or dining room, we heard the sound of footsteps coming up the front hall stairs and stopping at our door. Then we heard a key going inside the lock and turning, the door opening and closing, footsteps walking into our reception room, past the fireplace and down our inside hall toward the kitchen and dining room area. We would look up, expecting to see a family member and sometimes there was no one there. The footsteps always stopped at the kitchen threshold except for one time. One calm summer's day, my father was home by himself and enjoying the sun while sitting on the outside back porch doing a crossword puzzle. He had just washed his lunch dishes and hung the wet dish cloth on the spring of the screen door to dry. A short time later, the door opened wide and slammed shut with great force. He got up quickly, expecting to see a family member, but there was no one there. The spring on the screen door was jumping up and down and the dish cloth was swaying wildly. My father opened the screen door, went inside the house and walked from room to room and found no one there. That was the one time the visitor walked past the kitchen. It was a mystery until a few years later when my mother and I got a Ouija Board. We were sitting in the living room using it and my mother asked the board who is walking in the house. The Ouija Board spelled out "Charlotte". After that, we called the visitor "Charlotte". For years, whenever something happened in the house that we could not explain, we would say it must be Charlotte.

There were large iron radiators in each of the main rooms and sometimes, even in the summer, they would clang and bang as though heat were coming through, even though the valves were closed and the radiators were cold. One evening, as my mother and I watched television in the dining room/den, the wallpaper in the room began to peel off of the walls. The wallpaper had been on the walls for at least ten years and, all of a sudden, started to peel and actually fell to the floor. You could hear it peeling as though invisible hands were working to remove it.

TIME TRAVEL

I lived in the Cherry Street house until I got married in 1974. When my husband, Al, and I were engaged, we were visiting his parents in Florida for a few days. Early Sunday morning, which happened to be Father's Day, I heard my parents calling my name. They were saying "Donna, is that you, why are you home?" It woke me up and I realized I was not home, I was in Florida. It was so unusual that I wanted to make note of the time so I looked at the alarm clock and at my watch and it was seven fifteen. I called my parents a few hours later and my mother answered the phone. I asked her if anything unusual had happened recently, without me mentioning what I experienced that morning. She said that I had better talk with Daddy. My father got on the phone and told me that he and my mother were in the kitchen having breakfast when they heard someone walk up the outside hall front stairs, turn the lock with a key, open and close the front door, walk through the reception room, go into my room and shut the door. They then heard my voice. They called out "Donna, is that you, why are you home? You're supposed to be in Florida." They rushed down the hall, from the kitchen to my room, and found the door to my bedroom open with no one inside. I asked my father what time this happened and he said around seven fifteen.

THE BATH RUG

My parents lived in the Cherry Street house for thirty years. Eventually, they moved to my eldest sister's house, across the street, where they had their own first floor apartment. When they decided to move from Charlotte's house, more strange things occurred. One day, my father was preparing to wash the bathroom floor and picked up the small fluffy bath rug that was on the floor. He brought it into the living room and placed it on the wall to wall carpet to get it out of the way. When he retrieved the bath rug, hours later, he noticed it was quite wet though it had been dry when he placed it there. The next time he washed the bathroom floor, he again put the bath rug on the living room carpet and again it was wet when he went to get it hours later. He thought it was very strange and decided to do a test. One night, he put the dry bath rug on the wall to wall carpeting in the living room. The next morning when he went to check it, the bath rug was sopping wet. He tried this at least five more times over the next few months and, in each instance, the bath rug was very wet and the carpeting underneath was dry. They had no pets, there were no leaks and my parents were the only people living there. The room was completely dry except for the bath rug.

CHARLOTTE'S CALLING CARD

In 1991, we celebrated my mother's birthday at my eldest sister's house, directly across the street from where we had lived, and the landlady of our old house, who I had not seen for many years, was at the gathering. She said to me "Donna, your father mentioned Charlotte, over the years, whenever something unusual happened in the house and we also have had our share of strange events, one of which happened recently." The landlady went on to tell us that she had purchased a new Electrolux vacuum cleaner that spring. One day, while vacuuming the reception room in her first floor apartment, she made an interesting find. As the vacuum went over the area between the reception room and the front bedroom, she saw something being pulled out from underneath the threshold and she gently removed it. It was an old Victorian style Christmas card with a drawing of a child dressed in a snowsuit while pulling a Christmas tree. On the card was written "To Papa Colgan from Charlotte 12-25-21" which was seventy years earlier. The landlady went to her house, across the street, to retrieve the card, so that she could show it to me. She also brought over a 1907 newspaper article from the 'Somerville Journal'. The article described the house as being a surgical and convalescent hospital from 1899, run by a nurse superintendent named Hattie C. Wheet. It mentions the large sunny rooms and the operating room. I think I know why there were built-in cabinets with glass doors in some of the bedrooms as they probably were used to store medical supplies and linens. There were times, over the years, when I was outside and no one was home, I would look up at the third floor reception room window and see a woman dressed in white standing there. Per my request, the landlady allowed me to make copies of Charlotte's 1921 Christmas card and the 1907 newspaper article from the 'Somerville Journal'.

ANOTHER BEGINNING

If this were the end of the story, it would be considered another unusual tale passed down over the years. But this is not the end of the story, it is another beginning. In May 2008, I began working at a RE/MAX real estate office in Acton, Massachusetts. Our company had eleven locations and one of them was in Lexington, Massachusetts. One of the employees who worked there is a nice lady named 'R' and we spoke with each other a couple of times each week for a few months. One day 'R' asked me where I was from originally and I told her that I was from Somerville. She said that she was also from Somerville. She then asked me what part of Somerville and I said that it was near Porter Square. She said that she was from that area also. Then she asked me what street and I said "Cherry Street." She screamed with excitement and asked if I was Donna Grover and I asked her if she was 'R'. It turned out that we grew up in the same house at the same time, she on the first floor and me on the third floor. We had not seen or had contact with each other for over thirty years. We now used married last names so we did not realize our true identities for the first few months we had been speaking with each other. Also, we had not yet met, in person, at work, so we did not know what the other looked like. She told me that her father still owned the house and her mother had passed away and, of course, we started talking about Charlotte. She said that her father sometimes worked the night shift as a deputy fire chief and her mother would be home alone and every so often would hear footsteps going through their first floor reception room and past her bedroom. My family, on the third floor, would only hear the footsteps during the daytime. 'R' said that she was with her mother when she was vacuuming their reception room and 'R' was the one who picked up Charlotte's card as it was pulled from underneath the threshold. I asked her where the card is. She said it was framed and hanging in her father's apartment along with the 1907 newspaper clipping from the 'Somerville Journal'.

THE DAMON CONNECTION

I did research on the Cherry Street house and found that a man named Daniel Demmon (sometimes spelled 'Damon' in archived records) lived in the house in the 1880s. He became very wealthy in copper mining, banking and real estate. In 1888, he purchased a home at 128 Beacon Street in Boston, a building that is now part of Emerson College. He built a summer house in Weston, Massachusetts and eventually made that his permanent residence. That property is now the home of Regis College and Daniel Demmon's former summer house is now where the president of the college lives.

I would not have known anything about Daniel Demmon were it not for a remarkable coincidence. A few years ago, I happened to do a Google search for the Cherry Street, Somerville house and was more than surprised when an article came up about Regis College. The school issues a yearly brochure for incoming students and, by chance, in that particular year, it was about Daniel Demmon. It showed photos of the three properties he lived at including the house on Cherry Street.

    I e-mailed 'R' the research papers that I had accumulated about our Cherry Street childhood home. She said there was another Damon who lived there in the 1990s – Matt Damon, the actor. Matt Damon is from nearby Cambridge where Daniel Demmon (Damon) was originally from, over one hundred years earlier. A close relative of Matt's rented my family's old third floor apartment for about five years and Matt stayed there between movies when he hit the big time. I wonder if Matt heard the disembodied sound of footsteps, a key turning a lock or a door opening and closing.

CHAPTER 3

MY INVESTIGATIONS AT THE ISABELLA STEWART GARDNER MUSEUM

In May 2008, I was contacted by a well-known Boston radio talk show host who heard about me through others. Since he knows my son, Justin, he told Justin that he wanted to meet me and invited our family to his house for dinner a few weeks later. When we first arrived, we went to the kitchen for appetizers and he said he had heard that I was the 'Real Deal'. After some discussion, he asked what I saw about him. I immediately described a male relative and the bad accident he had while walking along a sidewalk many years before. I also saw a deceased female relative and the two medical conditions that she had. The talk show host buried his face in his hands, in amazement, and told us who these people were and confirmed that what I said was accurate. He asked me how I knew these things and I said that I did not know but that I saw them. After a few more stories, he asked if I would be interested in going to the Gardner Museum for a tour and to see if I sensed anything regarding the 1990 art heist. I agreed to help and he made the arrangements for us to go there.

On Sunday afternoon, August 10, 2008, my husband, Al, and I drove to the talk show host's house, as planned, and the host's wife drove us all to the museum where we met a couple who were to accompany us. It was a beautiful sunny day and we were met at the door by an investigator and given a grand tour of the museum. The investigator did not believe in psychics and, to him, this was not considered anything but a tour. There were many visitors at the museum that day and our group fit in as regular art lovers. I brought a steno pad and some pencils with me as I had read on the museum's website that pens were not allowed, the reason being that ink may accidently touch a valuable art object or the antique wallpaper.

When we entered the room called the 'Short Gallery', I came up with the name 'Richard' and the expression 'Smart Aleck'. The investigator was speaking with the talk show host and I politely interrupted them and asked if 'Richard' and 'Smart Aleck' meant anything. I was then told that one of the security guards on duty at the time of the robbery, March 18, 1990, was named 'Richard' and he was known as a 'Smart Aleck' in the police report and that no one knew that. I then asked if a small piece of paper had fallen off of the back of one of the stolen paintings during the robbery and I pointed to an area on the floor in the next room where I envisioned it to be. The investigator acknowledged that a label had fallen off of the back of one of the stolen paintings and was found on the floor at the precise area that I was pointing to. I then said that one of the robbers said something that a British person would say but that I could not think of the word so I said 'cheerio'. He said that one of the robbers called the other one 'mate'. I asked how he knew that and if the robbers were recorded. He would not answer my question and said he had his way of knowing. I found the answer to my question in Ulrich Boser's book 'The Gardner Heist' that came out six months later in February 2009. One of the guards, supposedly, heard one of the robbers call the other one 'mate'. The talk show host asked me about the condition of the stolen art and I told him that one of the paintings has a split in it. I was then told that one of the paintings is on wood and it does have a split in it.

We went to the main entrance of the inside garden and I was standing next to the lion statue that was located to my right. At that moment, I felt Mrs. Gardner rush over to me, hold my right arm and ask me to get 'Ellen' or a name that sounds similar. I asked the investigator if he recognized the name Ellen or a similar sounding name but he did not. Mrs. Gardner was showing me the Blue Room entry and told me that she was standing there when a robber went in and stole one of her paintings. She said that an alarm should have sounded but it did not. I found out later that there was an alarm over the Blue Room entry that the robbers disengaged. (Oil on canvas, 'Chez Tortoni' by Manet, was stolen from the Blue Room.)

I also learned of the strange occurrence that happened on Mrs. Gardner's birthday, April 14, 2008. The bust of a nun sculpture sits on the top of a cabinet that is in the Gothic Room. This is the same room where the life size painting of Mrs. Gardner, by John Singer Sargent, is on display. The nun had always faced the side of the room as Mrs. Gardner requested. When the security guard checked the room on his rounds early that morning, he noticed that the nun was facing the center of the room. The top of the cabinet was scratched where the nun sculpture had moved, seemingly on its own. The museum has the most sophisticated surveillance cameras but, for some reason, the nun sculpture was not seen moving.

After our tour, the talk show host treated our group to a wonderful lunch at the museum's café. When my husband and I returned home after the investigation, I exchanged emails with the investigator who had given us the tour. He asked if I would email him the list of items that I came up with during my visit. I not only sent him an email with my list of items, I also scanned and attached the steno pad pages that I wrote my notes on and I emailed a copy to the talk show host.

A few weeks after that first visit, I was contacted by the talk show host. He said that a reporter from the 'Boston Herald' newspaper wanted to go with me on another investigation to see how I 'do my thing'. Arrangements were made and the second investigation was on Thursday evening, October 9, 2008, when I was accompanied by my son Justin. We arrived early and found a parking space on Palace Road and waited inside the car. Shortly before our scheduled seven-thirty meeting, we walked through the small parking lot and went to the garden house door where we were told to meet the same investigator who accompanied me on my first tour. Right on schedule, he opened the door, greeted us and introduced a museum employee who was to accompany us as we walked through the museum. I suggested that we wait outside until the arrival of the talk show host's producer who was bringing four recording devices from the radio station. We waited outside for a short time until the producer arrived and then we all went inside the museum. The 'Boston Herald' newspaper reporter was on his way and arrived about an hour later. The museum employee was holding a pad of paper and walked along with us, taking notes, while she asked me questions about my visit in August. I told her about the experience I had when standing next to the lion statue on August 10th - how Mrs. Gardner grabbed my right arm and pleaded with me to get 'Ellen' or a similar sounding name. The employee said that was very interesting but I did not know how interesting until about an hour later when we visited the carriage house.

The carriage house was later torn down, in July 2009, to make room for the museum's new addition. The museum had to go to the Supreme Judicial Court of Massachusetts to get permission to tear it down and finally won approval. We went inside the carriage house but we could not go to the second floor apartment because an artist-in-residence was up there at the time of our visit. The employee then told us about the apartment. During a recent eight month period, there were five artists who lived there at different times and all of them experienced paranormal activity. The room and furniture, and even the bedding and curtains, would get electrified and unusual things would occur and one female artist had the same experience that I had. Many evenings, when she retired for the night, a woman would hold her arm, speak in her ear and plead with her to get 'Ellen'. I asked the employee who 'Ellen' was and the employee said 'Ella' was Mrs. Gardner's personal maid and whenever Mrs. Gardner wanted something, she would say "Get Ella." We were told that Mrs. Gardner's bedroom furniture was upstairs in the apartment and it was where the artist slept.

After leaving the carriage house, we walked back to the main building and went to the archive room. Outside the room was a small area that had some file cabinets and a fax machine. The employee told us what happened one evening, at about seventy thirty, when she was alone upstairs while working inside the room. She was sitting on the floor, going over some items, when she saw something move in front of her. She looked up and saw Mrs. Gardner standing in the doorway about ten feet away. She was wearing a long dark dress and her head had a bright glow around it. The apparition stayed for a few seconds then disappeared.

I was also told by the employee that, one evening, a very bright light came from the upstairs area that had been Mrs. Gardner's living quarters. The light seemed to be an entity and travelled down to the courtyard.

On my October 9, 2008 visit, I was showing the five people, that I was with, the nun sculpture that moved on top of the cabinet. We were standing in front of the cabinet and I started asking questions aloud such as "Is someone here that would like to make their presence known?" Suddenly, a Morse Code-like metallic tapping sound came from inside the closed cabinet and each of my questions was answered by this tapping sound. I asked the investigator if I could open the cabinet and he said "No." At that moment, the code-like tapping sound came out of the cabinet and settled on the large metal candelabra that stood in front of the cabinet. Again, with each question that I asked, I would get a response. The investigator walked around the area of the cabinet and candelabra and tried to reproduce the same tapping sound but it could not be done. Furthermore, we were all standing still when the sound came from the cabinet and the candelabra. We were looking for an explanation and thought the sound may have been caused by vibrations from traffic. We looked out the window and saw that there was very little traffic. I was quite surprised when I visited the museum in September 2009 and saw a large square object sitting on the floor next to the cabinet. It had the words 'Vibration Detector' on the top.

As we continued to walk through the museum, we came to a room on an upper floor with windows that looked out onto a balcony. The room seemed to be an office and had a round table and a desk. I asked if Mrs. Gardner died in the room and the employee acknowledged this was true and that it had been Mrs. Gardner's bedroom. The employee said that Mrs. Gardner enjoyed the views of Boston from this room.

Also, during my October 9, 2008 visit, I noticed a male figure hiding among the palm plants that were along the side of the room I was walking through. He was a condensed shadow in human form and was cautiously watching our group with interest. I told the others what I saw and, at that moment, the spirit realized that I could see him. He then came out from behind the shadows of the palm plants, extended a hand and asked me to follow him and that he would show me where a dead person was. I told the others what he was saying and I held his hand as we walked along with the group following us. We came to the end of the room and there was a large slab. I was then told that was where Mrs. Gardner was laid out for her funeral and that her casket had rested on top of the slab. The spirit was very kind and devoted to Mrs. Gardner.

On Sunday, April 4, 2010, I saw in the news that Robert Wittman, a retired FBI agent who worked on the Gardner Museum case, had written a soon to be released book 'Priceless'. The name 'Robert Wittman, FBI' sounded familiar and that is because it was among the notes that I wrote on the steno pad that I had with me on my August 10, 2008 visit to the museum. On one line, I wrote the name 'Robert'. On the next line under 'Robert', I wrote 'Whitcomb last name W' (The author's name is 'Wittman'). On the next line, I wrote 'FBI'.

Among the additional information from my steno pad, emails and other notes that has also proven to be accurate, is the following:

Robert – small crimes – Connecticut - Investigators searched the Connecticut property of mobster Robert Gentile looking for clues.

Barn-like structure with hidden underground chamber - I mentioned in an August 11, 2008 email to investigators that I saw a barn-like structure with a hidden underground chamber. A few years later, agents searched Robert Gentile's Connecticut property that included a shed with barn-like doors that was found to have a hidden area under the floor. There is a picture of the shed in the book 'Master Thieves' by three time Pulitzer Prize winning reporter Stephen Kurkjian, published in 2015. Also, among the names in his book is 'Daniel Falzon, FBI' who worked on the museum case. This is a name that I wrote on my steno pad during my first investigation of August 10, 2008.

Maine – restaurant – Robert - Investigators interviewed a mobster's widow who lives in Maine. She told them that, many years before, she and her husband, Robert Guarente, met Robert Gentile at a Maine restaurant and that they went out to the parking lot where her husband transferred some of the stolen paintings from his car to the trunk of Robert Gentile's car.

There are three robbers not two. – During my first investigation of August 10, 2008, I said that there were three robbers. After I said that, I was told that they thought there were two. They eventually realized that there were three.

Whitey Bulger – During my first investigation, on August 10, 2008, the talk show host asked me if gangster, Whitey Bulger, would ever be found. I said that he would be found in three years, living near water, and that he had a heart condition and needed access to a medical facility to obtain medicine. The talk show host then said that Whitey would be eighty-one when found, if my prediction came true. James 'Whitey' Bulger was captured on June 23, 2011 in Santa Monica, California at the age of eighty-one and it was made public that he had occasionally travelled to Mexico to obtain heart medicine.

Precognition of the Robbery

In the 1970s, I was working as the Concert Manager at New England Conservatory of Music in Boston and some of the conservatory students and faculty performed in concerts at the Gardner Museum. One day, in 1973, Johanna, the woman in charge of scheduling the museum concerts, asked me if I would fill in as a page turner at one of their concerts. This particular performance was a live radio broadcast with a well-known violinist from New York and his piano accompanist. As the page turner, I would sit next to the pianist and turn the pages of the sheet music while she played the piano. Johanna set up a time for me to stop by on a Saturday morning so that she could show me where they held their concerts and where I would be sitting. It was the first time that I had been to the museum and Johanna treated me to tea and cookies on Mrs. Gardner's china. I was intrigued by a certain oil painting and asked who it was and she told me it was a self-portrait of Rembrandt. I asked if I could touch it and she said that I could. I then asked if there was an alarm on it and she said there was not. I was surprised that such a valuable painting had no protection. I asked Johanna again if I could touch it and she said that I could, so I gently and quickly touched it and exclaimed that I had just touched a Rembrandt. Seventeen years later, that painting was taken off of the wall by the robbers who tried, but failed, to get it out of its heavy wooden frame and it was left on the floor.

My Isabella Stewart Gardner Museum Investigations

I was somewhat hesitant to make my Gardner Museum investigations public but, I know that by withholding my story, something would be missing from this historic case. I have extensive emails between certain investigators and myself as proof that my information led to the identities of two of the robbery suspects along with other important details. My hope is that by making my information public, it will help in the safe return of Mrs. Gardner's stolen treasures. There is much more to the Isabella Stewart Gardner Museum besides 'The Biggest Art Heist in History'.

My Childhood Home and Mrs. Isabella Stewart Gardner

My family moved to Cherry Street in Somerville, Massachusetts in October 1956 and lived there for thirty years. While doing research on the house, I found that there is a connection with the man who lived there, in the 1880s, and Isabella Stewart Gardner. His name was Daniel Demmon (sometimes spelled 'Damon' in public records). After Daniel became wealthy in banking, real estate and copper mining, he sold the Cherry Street house and moved to 128 Beacon Street in Boston. Isabella Stewart Gardner and her husband, Jack, lived at 152 Beacon Street. Jack Gardner also worked in banking, real estate and copper mining. Mrs. Gardner loved to entertain so it would not be surprising for Daniel to be among their guests, especially since both men were in the same businesses. I also learned that one of Daniel's two daughters, Abby Harding Demmon, married a man named William R. Gardner, though I do not know if this man was related to Jack Gardner.

Through further research, I found that after my parents moved out of the Cherry Street home, the brother of actor, Matt Damon, rented our old third floor apartment and Matt stayed there between movies. It was when he hit the big time with 'Good Will Hunting'. The Damons and Daniel Demmon were originally from the neighboring City of Cambridge.

Contact Five Years After My Investigations at the Gardner Museum

Five years after my investigations at the Isabella Stewart Gardner Museum, I received the following email from the museum employee who accompanied our group on the night of October 9, 2008, my second investigation at the museum. It relates to the turning nun statue and Ralph Waldo Emerson.

Sent: Monday, June 24, 2013 11:58 PM
Subject: I S G M

Dear Donna,

I just happened to stumble upon this blog entry re: your visit to the Gardner that one evening. I was actually looking to see if anyone had written about the turning nun bust - (there is a story circulating online about an Egyptian statue that has been turning on its own...)

It was good to read your account - I recall similar and many more details about our visit together that truly struck me. When we first met, at night, in the back garden, instead of saying hello to me you reached out your hand and said something like "Emerson would be a fine man to have dinner with" - I had been working / studying a manuscript of Emerson's over the last two days - no one could have known that. And then, you grabbed my hands and asked about Mrs. Gardner's dogs...do you remember this...?

Anyway, it was an unforgettable evening and I was interested to read your description. I no longer work at the Gardner, but have many memories.

Warm regards,
A legitimate source

CHAPTER 4

FINDING LOST VALUABLES

DIAMOND AND SAPPHIRE

In 1994, I began working at a large real estate office near Boston, Massachusetts and, as the weeks passed, my associates realized that I had a unique ability. The office manager noticed that the agents took up some of my time with their questions and conversations about the paranormal and she politely told me that if anyone should ask me questions on that subject, I was to tell them that I could only talk about it on my lunch hour because I had work to do.

One morning, about two weeks later, the manager came into my office and said "Donna, remember a few weeks ago when I asked you not to talk about the paranormal on company time? Well, forget about what I said." She then asked for my help in finding two valuable rings that her mother had left her. As I sat at my desk, I was transported to another dimension and immediately stood in the doorway of her bedroom. I saw her dresser against a far wall and walked over to it. There were three jewelry boxes on top of the dresser and I opened the drawer of one of the jewelry boxes. It was lined with light blue material and I described the pieces of jewelry that I saw inside. As I stood in front of her dresser, I sensed where her rings were. I told her to look in the back of a particular dresser drawer and that her rings were near a cloth that had a red Oriental design. I also saw a jewelry pouch with pearls.

On her way home, the manager thought about what I said regarding the red Oriental design cloth and she remembered that a friend had given her a scarf with that design a few years before. She looked in the back of the dresser drawer, that I mentioned, and found the scarf. She unfolded it and wrapped inside was a box and inside the box were her two rings.

An hour or so later, the manager came back to the office, stood outside and knocked on the large front picture window to get my attention while she held up her hand wearing the two rings. She said that the pouch with the pearls, that I saw, was in her safety deposit box at the bank where she had been that morning, before she came to the office to ask for my help in finding her rings. After that experience, it was okay for me to use my psychic gift in the office any time at all.

GOLD BRACELET

While at the same office, I received a call from a woman named Lorraine, an agent with another company and someone I did not know. She asked for my help in finding her gold bracelet. She got my name from Ms. S, a sales associate in my office who had asked for, and successfully received, my help in finding her own lost bracelet. Lorraine had placed an ad in the local newspaper offering a reward for its return. I told her that I would not accept a reward and would be happy to help find her bracelet.

After speaking with Lorraine and hanging up the phone, I sat at my desk and received visions in my mind as they came to me one by one. This time, I was not transported anywhere and I did not know what these visions meant. I first saw a gold cup then a large flat red object that looked like a book, yellow flowers, a small brown house and AX7. I called Lorraine and left her a voicemail with this information and said that I did not know if these things meant anything and that I would call her if I received more information.

The next day, it was my turn to fill in for the receptionist while she was at lunch and I was sitting at the front desk when Lorraine called. I answered the phone and she screamed with excitement that she had found her bracelet and that all of the things that I mentioned led to its discovery. She said that she used a section of her kitchen for her office and in the area was a big red appointment book and nearby were yellow flowers. There was also a miniature brown house near the book and next to the house was an American Express bill with AX7 on it. The gold cup that I saw was the gold pencil cup that sat amongst the other items. She looked inside the gold pencil cup and found her bracelet. She said that she had seven year old twins and one of them may have found the bracelet and put it inside the cup. Since I insisted I would not accept a reward, she came over to my office that afternoon with a huge bouquet of flowers to thank me.

MOTHER'S BRACELET

Ms. S, the woman who gave Lorraine my name, had asked for my help in finding her own lost bracelet. Ms. S was married with grown children and on a recent Mother's Day, they had given her a beautiful 'Mother's' bracelet with all of their individual birthstones. As Ms. S was in the office speaking with me, I was transported to her home where I saw a blue carpet and a desk. I focused on the right hand bottom drawer of the desk that had something to do with the letter 'P'. I told her that if she opened that drawer, she would find her Mother's bracelet. She said that her home office did have a blue carpet and a desk and she would look where I said she would find her bracelet. She went home right away and opened the bottom right hand drawer of her desk. There she found what she thought was an empty pretzel bag and was ready to throw it away but, before she did, she remembered my mentioning the letter 'P' so she looked inside the pretzel bag and found her bracelet. The next day, she came to work wearing her lost and found Mother's bracelet and ran over to show me and everyone else who was there.

HEART-SHAPED PENDANT

One day, in 1996, I received a call from D, an agent in my office. She said that she had searched her house for days and could not find her large gold heart-shaped pendant that hung from a heavy gold chain. It was a special piece of jewelry that she enjoyed wearing in the winter months and she thought she had stored it in a safe place.

After a few moments of our speaking on the phone, I found myself standing inside the entryway of her house. I saw a mahogany chest on the first floor and told her to open the drawer of the mahogany chest that held her white lace tablecloths. She then confirmed that her white lace tablecloths were in a mahogany chest. I had no idea where I was getting this information as I quickly received images in my mind. I had never been to her house and did not know what the interior or exterior of her house looked like. As we continued talking, I saw her running down the stairs while holding a phone to her ear and walking over to the mahogany chest. I told her to open the drawer that held the tablecloths and she did. She said that she saw the white lace tablecloths but did not see the pendant. I told her that if she lifted up the tablecloths, she would find the pendant underneath. She did as I asked and found her pendant underneath the white lace tablecloths. A few months later, I was invited to her house and it was exactly as I saw it in my mind that day.

THE ATTIC ROOM

In the late 1990s, I was at work and Ms. M, a long-time sales associate, asked for my help in finding her summer clothes. She said that people often ask me to find lost valuables but that her summer clothes were valuable to her. Almost immediately, I was transported to the sidewalk that runs in front of her house. As I walked along the sidewalk, I described to her, in detail, what I was seeing. I arrived at her house and stood facing the front of the house and walked up the front steps. The front door was wide open and I walked inside. The stairs, leading to the upper floors, were in front of me. I described the décor, furniture and flowers that I saw in the areas of the house that I could see as I walked up the stairs. I came to the second landing and continued walking up another level until I reached the attic. I stood at the threshold of the attic and looked inside. In the middle of the attic room, I saw a child's old small red wagon with a grey stripe along its side. I said that the grey stripe was once white. I saw a highchair near the right wall and yellow curtains on the floor on the left side of the room. I walked over to the curtains, picked them up and saw a plastic bag with her clothes inside. I told Ms. M that her summer clothes were under the curtains. Ms. M said she had looked there but had not seen them. I told her that the clothes were in a large plastic bag under the curtains and that the bag had a similar color as the curtains so they blended in and she missed seeing the bag. Ms. M went home, walked up to her attic, went to the left side of the room and found the yellow curtains on the floor. She picked the curtains up and saw the plastic bag I had described, looked inside the bag and found her summer clothes.

Ms. M said that there is an old small red wagon with a grey stripe sitting in the middle of the attic room as I had envisioned it. It was hers when she was a child and the stripe was white years ago. She also affirmed there is a highchair on the right side of the room. Since I have never seen her house, I should not have known what it looks like but I did. My visions were precise as I walked to her house, went inside and found what was missing. Ms. M still keeps in touch and has never forgotten the lost and found summer clothes.

VALUABLE PHOTOS

Ms. M called me a few years ago and, once again, asked for my help in finding something that was missing. She is the same woman that asked me to find her summer clothes about twenty years before. This time, she needed my help in finding lost photos that have great sentimental value to her family. She had brought the photos to a photo shop to have duplicates made. It is the same photo shop that she has done business with for many years. When she went to pick up the photos, they could not be located. Right away, I could see, in my mind, the photos being mistakenly put inside another customer's file. As I was telling her this on the phone, I did not know where the information was coming from and it was as though someone, who had knowledge of her missing photos, was talking through me. I then reassured her that her photos would be found and returned to her in a few months.

About two months later, Ms. M called me and said that her photos had been found. A customer had picked up her own photos that were in a large envelope. When she got home, she put them aside and had not opened the envelope until recently. What she found inside was not only her own photos but also Ms. M's originals. Fortunately, the customer brought them back to the photo shop and they were returned to Ms. M.

TIFFANY NECKLACE

In 2001, Ms. B, one of our agents, stopped by my office and asked if I could locate her daughter's missing Tiffany necklace. This particular necklace had a sterling heart charm that was engraved with the daughter's initials.

I had no idea what the daughter's home looked like but I was immediately transported to where she lived and walked over to a bookcase. I was drawn to a particular book with a red cover and I told Ms. B that if her daughter opened the book, she would find her missing necklace. Ms. B relayed my message to her daughter and, a few minutes later, the daughter called to tell her mother that she had found the necklace where I said it would be. She remembered she had been reading that book with the red cover and somehow her necklace had fallen off and landed between the pages. She could not believe her eyes when she found the book exactly where I said it would be, opened it and discovered her Tiffany necklace with the sterling heart charm, engraved with her initials.

MOVING DAY

My psychic gift often came in handy at work, since I had contact with many people, directly and indirectly. It was only a matter of time before I would be asked, once again, to help find something. On this particular occasion, I received a call from one of our top agents, D, who is the same woman who asked for my help in finding her gold heart-shaped pendant. She had been at a house closing that day and was on her way back to the office when she received a call from the woman who had just purchased the house. The moving van had brought over the family's furniture and other belongings, unloaded the truck and carried everything into the house. The woman and her husband had already spent three hours organizing and putting things away but there was one thing they could not find. It was a special irreplaceable set of white dishes. The woman thought that the movers had lost them and was panicking. D told her that she would call me to see if I knew where the dishes could be. D called me at the office while she had the woman on hold on another line. Immediately, I saw where the dishes were even before I was transported to the front door entrance. I walked through the living room, toward the kitchen, and I saw a pantry with boxes on the floor. I walked over to the boxes and saw that one was smaller than the others and I knew it was the one with the white dishes. Since the smaller box was surrounded by a group of larger boxes, it could be overlooked. The top of the smaller box was closed and sealed with masking tape but I could see the white dishes inside without opening the box. I told D to tell the woman to look in her pantry and she will find her dishes in the smallest box on the floor. Sure enough, the woman went to the pantry, found the box, opened it and her special irreplaceable set of white dishes was inside.

KODAK MEDALLION

My husband, children and I were in Rochester, New York for a family wedding in the 1990s and that is where we met Bill. Bill and his wife are acquaintances of my husband's sister, Iris, and we were all seated at the same table during the reception. Bill had worked at the Kodak Company in Rochester and received a gold medallion upon his retirement. He had not seen the medallion for many years and had no idea where it was. Iris told him that I was psychic so Bill asked me if I could help locate his medallion. All of a sudden, I was standing in front of his bureau and could see inside a particular drawer without opening it. I told Bill that his medallion was wrapped up in a red cloth in the back left hand side of his top bureau drawer. Later that evening, my husband, three children and

I were at our hotel when Iris called. She wanted me to know that Bill had just arrived home, opened the top bureau drawer of his dresser, looked in back on the left side, found the red cloth and wrapped inside was the Kodak gold medallion. He called Iris and asked her to thank me for finding his lost and found retirement treasure.

PSYCHIC GPS

A few years ago, my son, Justin, called to relay a message from a real estate agent whom I did not know. She had heard that I was psychic and hoped that I could help find her purse. She had parked her car and inadvertently left her purse inside while she showed a property that day. When she went back to the car, her purse was missing. As Justin and I spoke on the phone, he had the woman on another line. I started to see visions, in detail, including an area of Boston that I was not familiar with. I was in spirit form and floating above the road and traffic as I traveled the route to find her purse. I saw a small business area off of a main street and described some of the businesses. I went around to the back of the businesses and saw a dumpster. I then brought my spirit down and stood on the ground, and then walked, as I searched the area where I knew her purse would be found. I then saw it next to the dumpster. The purse was open and I saw a wallet inside. In spirit, I picked up the wallet and saw that the money and credit cards had been removed but the IDs were still there. The woman was not sure of the area but would follow my directions of how to get there using the signs and landmarks that I saw in my travel. The woman drove about eight miles and came upon the business area that I described and drove around to the back. The dumpster was there, as I saw it, and she noticed what looked like a purse lying on the ground next to the dumpster. She got out of her car, walked over to the dumpster and picked up her purse. Inside was her wallet with her

IDs but her money and credit cards were gone. I have no idea how I was able to pinpoint exactly where her purse would be found.

CHAPTER 5

PREDICTING THE FUTURE

THE POPE WAS SHOT

On May 12, 1981, I was a young married woman with two small children and worked for a temporary employment agency. One of my work assignments was in a first floor office at Newton Wellesley Hospital in Newton, Massachusetts. At the time, I had worked there, off and on, for about six months. The room I walked through, to get to my office, was occupied by a large three-sided desk where a group of telephone operators sat answering the incoming calls. As the months went by, the women became aware of my psychic abilities when I told them accurate things about themselves and their families. It was daily entertainment and nothing more until one particular day. I was working at my desk and had a vision that Pope John Paul was going to be shot within twenty-four hours. I was not 100% sure if this would actually happen and tried to put it out of my mind but the vision kept coming back with a feeling of uneasiness. I felt that he would be seriously wounded but that he would be okay. I realized that if I did not tell someone and it did happen, I would not be able to prove that I had predicted it.

I left my office and went to the room where the women sat around the large desk. I told them of my vision of the Pope being shot within twenty-four hours and that I prayed he would be safe. There was nothing else I could do. If I told the authorities, they would think I was crazy and then if the Pope was really shot, they would wonder how I could possibly know that would happen.

The next day, on May 13, 1981, I was in my office working and a hospital employee, from another department, came running down the hall and ran into the switchboard room. She had just heard on the radio that the Pope had been shot. The women were stunned and said that I had predicted it. I do not know how I knew what would happen to the Pope but I did and I am thankful that he survived.

WORLD OF MUSIC

Sarah and I were co-workers at a real estate office in Wellesley, Massachusetts in the 1990s. She was in the marketing department and responsible for doing the newspaper ads, brochures and feature sheets for the many real estate agents we worked with. She was originally from New York and she and her husband, Ben, moved to the Boston area when he began working for a computer company many years before.

Sarah and I loved going for walks on our lunch hour and we would often cross the street to the campus of Wellesley College and follow the foot paths that threaded the area. It was a luxury to get up from our desks and get some fresh air in such a pretty place with its peaceful pond, hundred year old trees and buildings where so many young ladies lived and studied and went off to save the world. Sarah and I were quite the pair and sometimes we would sit on a bench, look out on the pond and watch the ducks paddle back and forth. A few times, we brought our lunches and sat on the grass and had a picnic.

Sarah had been worried about her husband's job as his company had been cutting back and one day he was told what he dreaded to hear. It was quite traumatic for the two of them because they had left New York where their family and friends lived and moved hundreds of miles away, settling in a new place, buying a house and raising their children. On one of our lunch time walks, Sarah told me what had happened and asked what I saw for their future. I told her that in August of that year, her husband would get a good job offer in the music business and that they would move back to New York. She thought it strange that I saw the music business since it was quite different from what he had been doing for many years.

As the weeks went by, Sarah thought about what I had predicted and wondered if this would actually happen. As more time went by, her husband got a call from a friend who had started a small business in Florida a few years before. It involved making tapes of party music that he sold to people for birthdays, holidays and other celebrations. The small business grew to be very successful and he realized he needed a large space to accommodate the growth. Since Sarah's husband had been a successful business manager at the computer company, this friend asked if he would work for the music company that would be moving from Florida to New York in August. It was very short notice but Sarah's husband accepted the offer and they moved to New York to start his new job. Meanwhile, they put their Boston suburban home on the market and Sarah stayed a few months longer until the home sold. The last I heard from Sarah, she and her husband were enjoying their new found lifestyle of dinner parties and mingling with show biz people and happy to be home in New York among their family and long-time friends.

DEAR MINDY

I was introduced to Mindy and Jane at a family wedding reception in Rochester, New York in the early 1990s. I had never met them before and knew nothing about them, only that they were guests at the wedding. They heard that I was psychic and invited me to sit down at their table and tell them what I saw about them. I told Jane that I saw two little blond girls standing next to an older man in a living room and that there was a large framed picture of palm trees hanging on the wall. I said that the man's name is Earl and that he is bad. Jane said that I was describing her grandfather Earl standing next to her two younger blond sisters. She said that he had a large picture of palm trees hanging on his living room wall and that he was convicted of molesting her two little sisters many years ago.

I also told Jane that she was married once before and it did not work out and that five years later she married her present husband. I said that she and her husband were planning to move to Ohio because of his work. Jane said that she had been married once before, was divorced and met her present husband five years later. He recently received a promotion at work and it required them to move to Ohio and they had just begun researching places to live to be near his new job.

I then looked at Mindy who was sitting across from me. I said that doctors had told her that she and her husband could never have children. She then told me that they had been to many fertility specialists and they all agreed that they could never have a child. I then told her that they would have a beautiful baby girl in eight years and that she would be a gift from God and recognized for her artistic talent. I told Mindy the name of her high school boyfriend and that he drove a red sports car and about the time he was upset when the car was in a minor accident. I told her about the health of her mother, the death of her father and other things that proved to be accurate.

In 2011, I received a message from Mindy. She had been searching for me for many years and did not know my last name. She finally made contact with someone who had been in the wedding party of twenty years before, where Mindy and I originally met. That person gave her my e-mail address and Mindy sent me this message:

"Hi Donna. I met you in the 90's at your friend's wedding. You shared so many things with me at that time that came to be with incredulous accuracy. I just reached out to your friend last night trying to find you, because I've thought about you so often over the years and she got me here. I would love to chat with you and share all of the events with you. Could we somehow do that? You are utterly amazing. Thank you."

A few days after receiving Mindy's email, we spoke on the phone at length and she told me of the many things I predicted that came true since we had met twenty years before. She and her husband had the beautiful baby girl, eight years later, as I predicted. She was now twelve years old. Her name is Mikayla which means 'Gift from God'. Mikayla had recently won recognition in a national contest for designing an evening gown that was chosen to be worn for a major charity event. Mindy emailed me the news article that has a picture of Mikayla receiving her award.

NIMBLE THIMBLE

I worked in the same office building in Wellesley, Massachusetts for fifteen years, from 1979 through 1994, and knew most of the wonderful people from the various offices. One of the businesses was a tailor shop called 'Nimble Thimble' that was owned by two dear ladies, Edda and Dahlia. They each had their own table and sewing machine that they worked at and Edda had an adorable apricot Toy Poodle, named Gonzo, who happily spent most days in a doggy bed under her table. Edda and Dahlia were always a joy and I looked forward to visiting them each day.

One day, Dahlia asked me if her son and his wife would have more children. They already had a little boy and I told her that they would have twin girls with 'A' names within two years. I even told her the week they would be born. She decided not to say anything about my predictions to her son or his wife.

The next year, Dahlia found out that her daughter-in-law was pregnant and, months later, she learned that she was carrying twins. Her granddaughters, Amy and Amanda, were born the exact week that I predicted. About three years later, I was at the July 4th parade in Natick, a neighboring town where I live. I was sitting on a bench in the town common with my husband, Al, and we saw a young man walking towards us with beautiful twin girls. I complimented him on his pretty girls and asked him their names. He said they were Amy and Amanda. I told him that a friend of mine, who lives in Wellesley, has twin granddaughters named Amy and Amanda. He said I was talking about his mother Dahlia.

On another visit to Nimble Thimble, I told Dahlia that a man she knows, in Italy, will break his leg while cutting down a tree. That evening, Dahlia received a phone call that a relative who lives in Italy broke his leg that day while cutting down a tree.

Predictions of true events were a common routine on my visits to the tailor shop. More importantly, Edda and Dahlia turned a routine work day into something special each time that I entered their shop. The little bell on their door, the Toy Poodle, Gonzo, greeting me and the warm smiles will remain with me forever. Thank you Edda, Dahlia and Gonzo.

FUTURE SON AND DAUGHTER

Ann was the mortgage broker in the real estate office where I worked in the mid-1990s. At the time, she and her husband had a beautiful three year old daughter. One day, Ann asked me if they would ever have more children. I told her that I saw a handsome blond baby boy, dressed in an undershirt and diaper, sitting on her knee. I predicted that she would tell me she was pregnant the next year around the holidays - almost two years in the future. I also told her that she and her husband would have a third child, a girl, and that I saw 'May'.

The week before Thanksgiving, the following year, I was downstairs in the kitchen, at work, when Ann came in and told me that she had just found out she was pregnant. She said she wanted me to be one of the first to know. As predicted, she had a beautiful baby boy with blond hair. Months later, I left that office to work elsewhere and had not seen Ann for several years. One day, I was in the area and walked by the office. Ann happened to be in the front reception room and ran out to greet me and gave me a hug. She said she had the third child that I predicted, a girl, and she called her May. It turns out that she was named after Ann's mother. I had no knowledge of Ann's mother's name at the time of my predictions.

TWIN BOYS

While working at a real estate company, I was often hired to play the piano at events such as open houses, bridal showers, retirement parties and holiday gatherings. One such function was a wedding cocktail hour at the Four Seasons Hotel in Boston. The bride, Mary, was an executive at the company I worked for and was a friend of Ann's, the mortgage lady that I accurately predicted would have a baby boy and girl. As I sat at the piano, Ann and two of her co-workers came over and asked me to predict if and when Mary, the bride, would have children. I told them that I saw twin boys who would be born in February, almost two years in the future. I said that they would be premature and that one would have a lung problem and the other would have a heart problem but that these problems would go away and they would be healthy after a hospital stay of a couple of weeks.

The next year, Ann contacted me and said that she had just received a call from Mary telling her that she was expecting twins. As I predicted, the twin boys were born prematurely in February and one had a lung problem and one a heart problem but everything turned out fine and they were healthy when they went home a few weeks later.

THE HORSE RACE GENTLEMAN

Let me preface this section by saying that I am not interested in horse racing and I know very little about it. On April 1, 2010, I received an e-mail from a gentleman named Hugh Mitchell, a retired copy editor for a Boston newspaper. He wrote a book entitled 'Dream Horses', in which he described his psychic ability to predict horse race winners. Hugh heard about me from one of his relatives, Margie Mitchell, who is a friend of mine.

In one of the first e-mails that Hugh sent to me, he asked if I was able to predict horse race winners. I told him that someone had asked me the same question once before. It was back in the late 1990s when I was working at a real estate office in Wellesley, Massachusetts. One of the sales agents, Larry, asked me if I could predict the winner in one of the horse races at that time. I told Larry that I saw the name 'Sonic Boom'. I said that this horse had not yet been born but I predicted that about ten years into the future, Sonic Boom would win many races and bring great wealth to his owners. Hugh e-mailed me back and said that my vision from the late 1990s had come true. In 2009, a horse, named Sonic Boom, won five races in a row in India. Hugh mailed me a copy of a newspaper article with the details.

Hugh asked me to try to predict some winners in the United States. On April 2, 2010, I told him that I saw the name 'Bon-Bon' or a name like candy. He said that a horse named 'Sidney's Candy' was expected to run in the Kentucky Derby. On May 1, we agreed that this must be the horse with the 'name like candy' that I envisioned. Hugh asked me which race Sidney's Candy would win, but unfortunately, I could not be sure about the answer to that question.

A few weeks later, I did predict the winner of the Kentucky Derby. On April 23, 2010, I emailed Hugh that the horse that would win has a name with a 'u' as a second letter and 'er' at the end. Hugh said that one of the horses had both of the credentials I mentioned: 'Super Saver'. Super Saver was indeed the winning horse that year. I also mentioned to Hugh that I saw the words 'devil's rainbow'. He said that I was probably thinking of the one filly in the field whose name was 'Devil May Care'.

On November 2, 2010, Hugh sent me an email asking which horse would win the Breeders' Cup Classic at Churchill Downs. He said that one filly, Zenyatta, was running against a bunch of Grade 1 male horses but Zenyatta was no ordinary filly. She had run nineteen times and won all nineteen races. Churchill Downs would be her twentieth and final race before retirement. If she won, she would have accomplished something that no other horse, male or female, had ever done before: win twenty straight races and retire undefeated.

I told Hugh that I saw a young male horse, light tan in color, running ahead of Zenyatta in the race. In the same vision, I recall seeing patches or pockets, small swaths of material, gingham, something country style and colorful. I saw long tables with food, corn on the cob, green grass, and people standing around having a nice time. Hugh emailed me the following message on November 8, 2010. "Donna, Congratulations. Zenyatta was indeed beaten by a younger male horse. It was a little difficult to tell the winning horse's color from the pics I've seen, but it does look to be lighter than Zenyatta. It was very exciting with Zenyatta coming up from last place in the stretch and losing by only a few inches. That foresight of yours is amazing. It was like watching a bit of film, without words."

CHAPTER 6

MAKING CONTACT

I SPOKE IN GERMAN AND WROTE IN POLISH

This case has left a lasting emotional impression on me and I, sometimes, find it difficult to talk about. At the time of the occurrence, in the 1970s, I was working as the Concert Manager at New England Conservatory of Music in Boston. I was on my lunch break in the lady's lounge that is off of the main concert hall, Jordan Hall. There was a fireplace, couch, some cozy chairs and a few small tables. It was a quiet day and I was by myself. I had a deck of playing cards and was trying to guess which card would come up as I pulled each one from the top of the deck. A lady entered the lounge, introduced herself as Lydia and asked me what I was doing and I told her. I had seen her a few times from a distance, down the hall, and I thought she may be a new employee or teacher. She asked me if I read cards and I told her that I did not but that I see images in my mind. She asked if I saw anything about her and, almost immediately, I said that I saw a word that did not look English. She told me to write it down and handed me a pen and piece of paper. She watched as I wrote the word 'Piotr'. She then told me that I had just written down her father's name in Polish and asked me what I saw about him. I said that I saw her father with valuable coins in his pocket that were being taken away and I saw barbed wire. She then told me that her father was captured by the Nazis and they took his valuable coins from his pocket and that he was put in a concentration camp where he died.

The rest of the lunch hour went by quickly and I envisioned many things from Lydia's life. She asked if I would continue my reading one day after work so, a few days later, we took the subway to where she lived which was off of Commonwealth Avenue. As soon as I walked inside her apartment, I said "A young woman lives here, she is pregnant and not married." Lydia looked at me and said that she did have a roommate who was pregnant and not married. She asked how I knew about her roommate and I told her that I did not know but that I could see her, though Lydia and I were the only ones inside the apartment.

Lydia and I sat at her kitchen table for over three hours and I told her life story in detail from the time she was a little girl living in Poland. I mentioned the name Edmund and described a young man with blond hair that was parted a certain way. I saw him dressed in a military uniform and that he had a letter from his mother, with blood on it, when he was found. She went into her bedroom and brought out a large gold framed picture of her brother Edmund, exactly as I described him, dressed in uniform with his blond hair parted a certain way. She then said he was found dead on a battlefield with a letter from their mother in his pocket

At the end of my three hours of spiritual communication, I said something that I did not understand and Lydia began to cry. I asked her what was wrong and she said that I had just spoken in German and given her a message from her best friend, Anna, who was fifteen years old the last time that Lydia saw her. At the time, Anna was being driven away on the back of a truck and, at that last moment, so many years before, Anna yelled to Lydia that if there was ever any way she could reach her, she would, and she did - through me. She spoke through me and said in German "This is Anna, I am reaching you now." Anna used me to get this message to her best friend Lydia, proving that there is an afterlife. It also shows that this dear friend, who died in a concentration camp, was waiting all these years to find someone that she could communicate through and somehow that person would be in contact with Lydia. I can still envision Anna on the back of the truck, her dark hair disheveled, the panic in her eyes, the torment on her face and her hands outstretched to a world she was trying to hold on to. I do not understand or speak the German or Polish languages but somehow I was able to bypass what I did not know so that I could relay a message from the other side.

PARANORMAL ACTIVITY – GILMANTON IRON WORKS

This is the first house in which I may have unintentionally caused paranormal activity to occur. My cousin, Charles William (Bill) Krug, was an artist who worked for an advertising agency in Laconia, New Hampshire in the 1970s. He was fascinated by the paranormal and loved telling his younger cousins ghost stories as we sat around his living room in the evenings. He was a member of a local acting group and he, my sister Bess and I would sometimes take turns reading parts from play manuscripts. My family and I visited Bill and his mother, our dear Aunt Kit, several times a year and we always had a great time.

During one of our visits, Bill brought me to the advertising agency where he worked and introduced me to Karen, one of his co-workers. Karen was also interested in the paranormal and had heard from Bill that I was psychic. Karen, her husband, Tom, and their two teenage children lived in an antique house in Gilmanton Iron Works, New Hampshire, not far from an old cemetery. Part of the house was built in the late 1700s and an addition was added a century later. Gilmanton Iron Works is where Grace Metalious, the author of the scandalous novel 'Peyton Place', lived. She used Gilmanton Iron Works as the town model for 'Peyton Place'.

Karen invited Bill and me to dinner at their house and was eager to test my psychic skills. After dinner and general conversation, Karen, Bill and I moved to the family room and sat at a rectangular-shaped wooden table that had a bench on each side. Karen's husband was a skeptic and preferred observing from his easy chair in the nearby living room. Karen and Bill sat across from me and they took turns writing words on pieces of paper to see if I could tell them what the words were. One of them would write a word, show it to the other, then fold up the paper and concentrate on the word. For some reason, I could never 'see' what Bill wrote but if he showed the word to Karen and she concentrated on it, I would 'see' the word and tell them what it was. It was interesting and showed that Karen and I were telepathically connected. I then took a large piece of paper and printed out the letters of the alphabet and the numbers 0 through 9. I then printed the word 'Yes' in the top right corner and the word 'No' in the top left corner, similar to a Ouija Board. I asked Karen for a piece of heavy thread and something I could use for a pendulum. She found a large marble-like bead and I put the thread through the hole in the bead and pulled it so that the thread was about eight inches long and made a knot at the end. I held the thread, with the bead, over the paper and we started asking questions to see if anything would happen. We each took turns with the pendulum and I had the most luck in getting results. I said that if the pendulum swung a certain way, we should follow to where it leads and if it stops on a letter or number or 'Yes' or 'No', to wait and see if it circles around that object. It was amazing that it actually worked. At that time, it was all fascinating entertainment and nothing more. We did not understand any of it and why it worked – it just did.

The pendulum swung and circled the letters, numbers, 'Yes' and 'No' to reveal many facts about people and things that only Karen knew and somehow I was the one spelling out these facts with the pendulum. I suspect that I was reading Karen's mind and unconsciously moving the pendulum myself to spell out what I was picking up from Karen. After a fun and very interesting evening, Bill and I said good-night to Karen and Tom.

A few days later, I was back home in Somerville when Bill called. He said Karen related to him that unusual activity was now occurring at the house. Doors opened and closed on their own, lights went off and on without anyone near a light switch and, in three of the rooms, drawers opened and objects were taken out and strewn around. This continued for many weeks and was very frightening to Karen, Tom and their children. Apparently, we stirred up a form of energy in the house that we did not intend to activate. At the time, it was all good-natured and we did not realize or expect that what we were doing was anything extraordinary.

Unfortunately, the paranormal activity at Karen's and Tom's house became so unbearable that they eventually sold the house and moved. Aunt Kit and Cousin Bill passed away in 1977 and I have not had contact with Karen or her family since. I will always remember that evening as a lesson that my psychic gift is not to be taken lightly. It was a learning experience for a student of the paranormal and I realize I must always tread with caution and expect the unexpected.

HAUNTED HOUSE – BELFAST, MAINE

I met my friend, Terri Messina, when we were working for an insurance company in Boston, right out of high school, before we decided what we wanted to do with the rest of our lives. She eventually graduated from nursing school and was a nurse for many years. We had many happy times together and she was the maid-of-honor at my wedding. She had a wonderful family and we often got together for special occasions. Terri's sister, Josie, was a few years older than Terri and was married with three young children. Each summer, Josie, her husband, Jim, and their children went to

Belfast, Maine for two weeks to house sit their relatives' beautiful estate that sat on eighty-eight acres of mostly woodland. Josie's sister-in-law was an artisan who made lovely ceramics and fine jewelry and needed someone to tend her store while she was away. There were also some hens, roosters and a few sheep on the property that needed daily attention. The estate consisted of a large 1790s white Colonial with black shutters, a smaller building, used as the store, and a barn.

One year, Josie invited Terri and me to accompany her family on their two week excursion and we all looked forward to having a fun time. When we arrived at the house, Josie's sister in-law, brother-in-law and their two teenage children greeted us warmly and had a delicious dinner prepared. We had a wonderful time that evening, singing songs of long ago as I played the old upright piano that sat in their living room. The in-laws were leaving the next morning and filled us in on what was needed to make sure everything ran smoothly while they were away.

As the days went by, nothing seemed out of the ordinary until later the first week. Terri and I shared a bedroom and one night a noise woke both of us up at the same time. The strong floral scent of perfume filled the room and I saw the shadowy form of a woman in a long dress standing at the nightstand that stood between our beds. The form dissipated within a few seconds and I reached over to the nightstand and turned on the light. Terri and I were both frightened and stayed up the rest of the night with all the lights in the room on. The next morning, we told Josie and Jim what had happened. Josie was very interested but Jim would have nothing to do with such foolishness. Josie admitted that she had a similar experience two summers before and, since then, she felt uneasy being there. She was now convinced that there was a ghostly presence and she would not go anywhere in the house alone.

One evening, with the three children safely asleep, Josie, Jim, Terri and I sat on the living room floor playing cards. Josie asked me to use my psychic ability and tell her things that came to mind. I started saying names and nicknames of people that I did not know and private things about these people that only Josie and her husband would know. They were amazed that I was getting this information from somewhere because I certainly would never know otherwise. I then said that something was going to happen at ten o'clock that evening. I had no idea what was going to happen at ten o'clock but I knew that it had to do with the house. We were intrigued but made light of the fact. We agreed that we would all meet in the living room well before ten o'clock to see what awaited us, if anything.

At a quarter to ten, we were again all sitting on the living room floor, looking at our watches and the antique clock that hung on the wall. The clock's pendulum swung back and forth and counted down each second as the minute hand got closer to ten o'clock. Only five more minutes, only one more minute, seconds to go…get ready. As the hour hand was on the ten and the minute hand struck the twelve, a huge bang reverberated throughout the house. It sounded like something large had slammed against the outside of the house. At exactly the same time as the huge bang sound, all the lights went out in the house. We could not believe what had just happened and even Jim was apprehensive. He got a flashlight and went outside to see if something had fallen against the house. He walked around the house exterior and came back in and said he did not see anything that may have fallen against the house. A little while later, we found that the water was no longer working in the house. None of us slept well that night and were shaken by what we had experienced.

The next morning, at exactly ten o'clock, the electricity and water came back on. Terri and I took a walk to the general store and we mentioned to the store's owner, and a few customers, what had happened at the house. We asked if anyone else had experienced electrical or water problems the previous evening and we were told that none had.

If it was a spirit that caused this to happen, I think they had a great sense of humor. I can imagine the spirit watching and waiting for us to jump at its practical joke. If it was a joke, apparently the 'ghost' gave me the information to pass on to the others that something would happen at ten o'clock the night before. The rest of our stay was uneventful but we were on alert for anything unusual until we were safely on our way home.

GUIDING A SPIRIT TO THE LIGHT

August 7, 2001 was a very hot day in the Boston area with temperatures over 100 degrees. I was at work and a colleague, Alice, received a telephone call from a frightened young woman that had moved into a house that Alice sold her the previous year. The first question the caller asked Alice was "Is my house haunted?" Alice is a refined, attractive, no nonsense woman with a logical mind and she was not prepared for such an unusual question. Not every real estate office has a resident psychic and, though unusual, my abilities have been called upon and used to a great extent over the years.

The caller, Sandra, lived in the house with her husband and their nine month old daughter. Alice put down the phone and walked over to my office and asked if I would help Sandra. At that moment, I envisioned a man of ethnic appearance that was no more than five feet, six inches tall. Alice picked up the phone and told Sandra of my vision. Sandra said that she was seeing the apparition of a man. Sandra asked if I would go to her house and I told her that I could go there that afternoon at four o'clock and I asked Alice to go with me.

When Alice and I arrived at the house, we were greeted by Sandra, who was waiting outside with her baby. I walked around the exterior of the house to sense anything unusual. It was a lovely older white Dutch Colonial in a nice area with a church across the street. A priest from the church had recently been called to the house for his assistance. He blessed the house but the paranormal activity continued.

Sandra invited us inside and we went into the living room. I sat on the love seat and Alice and Sandra sat on the couch. Sandra was very apprehensive about her experiences and needed to talk with someone who would believe her. I asked Sandra to sit next to me and she came over and sat down on the love seat. I held her hand and asked her exactly what she had been seeing and how many times she had seen this figure. She said it was a mist that took on the shape of a man, that she had seen it about ten times but that the last time it looked hideous. I asked her why it looked hideous and she said it looked distorted. I told her that it looked that way because it had not finished materializing into a human form. I also told her that she was psychically gifted and that the spirit she was seeing was someone that wanted to communicate with her and that she should not be afraid. This gave her comfort and assurance that what she was experiencing was not to be feared.

I asked Sandra if I could walk through each room to try to get a sense of paranormal activity and she agreed. She picked up the baby and she and Alice followed me from room to room on the first and second floors. As I walked through each room, I told Sandra where I felt the man's presence. I said he was often in the kitchen and spends time in the baby's room and in the computer room. Sandra said that those were the three rooms she saw him in. He was mostly seen in the kitchen and a few times she saw him in the baby's room. She also saw his misty form in the computer room where her husband had his office. Her husband would sometimes feel the presence of someone standing behind him as he sat working at his desk but, when he turned around, there was no one there.

We went back to the living room and I sat on the love seat by myself, Alice sat on the couch, and Sandra sat on the floor with the baby. Immediately, I felt the presence of the man, his energy and his emotions. I said he died at the age of fifty-seven of a heart attack in his kitchen five years before. I said that he smoked and owned a small brown boat. I saw him dressed in new clothes – black pants and a glowing white dress shirt. He was carrying a stack of men's folded new glowing white shirts and was walking towards a shelf as though to place the shirts there. He was crying and said he loved his son, Sandra and his granddaughter and he wanted to be near them. With a great sense of relief, Sandra realized who I was talking about. It was her father-in-law who she had never met. He died of a heart attack in his kitchen in his home in Columbia at the age of fifty-seven, five years before. He was no more than five feet, six inches tall, he smoked, he had a small brown boat and owned a men's clothing store. Sandra got up from the floor and walked over to a table that was against a wall. She opened a drawer, took out a photo album and showed Alice and me a picture of her father-in-law. He was standing next to his small brown boat.

I told Sandra that her father-in-law was happy now that he was finally able to communicate with her. I asked her if she wanted him to leave and she said that he could stay. I told her that he should pass over and that I had to speak with him privately. I got up from the love seat and walked into the hall and stood next to the stairs that went to the second floor. I told him that Sandra said that he could stay and that she, his son and his grandchild loved him. I informed him what year it was and that he was no longer living and should pass through the light where many of his loved ones are. I felt his strong emotions of love for his family and sadness in his acceptance that he was no longer living and he was crying through me. After a few moments, he went to the light and was gone. I knew he had passed over when the strong emotions suddenly stopped and there was silence and a great sense of calm.

I walked into the living room where Sandra, the baby, and Alice were waiting. They had heard what I said to Sandra's father-in-law as I stood in the hall next to the stairs. A great burden was lifted from Sandra's shoulders and she was overjoyed that I was able to solve a most unusual case of paranormal activity. I was at my office the next day and received a call from Sandra. She thanked me and said she was in such a fragile state when we said good-bye, the previous day, that she forgot to ask me how much I charge for my services. I told her that I do not charge anything and that I was happy that I was able to help her. She insisted that she pay me and I insisted that I would not accept payment. Sandra showed up at my office a short time later to thank me in person and gave me a gift of imported candies in a lovely decorative tin. I still have the tin as a keepsake. She said she would never forget what I did and how much she appreciated it. I was happy to help a young family in need and, in doing so, I made direct contact with the spirit of a kind man who died before he could enjoy his extended family that he watched over and loved.

DEAD MAN IN GARAGE

On the evening of December 8, 2010, I was the guest speaker at a 'Mystery Writers of America' meeting at the Brookline Public Library. Among those in attendance, was a group of friends of my son Justin and his girlfriend Laura. I was introduced to Rachel, who was the only one in the group that I had not met. The group asked what I saw about Rachel and I said that I saw 'Ed'. Rachel said that she did not know anyone named 'Ed' and asked what I saw about him. I said "He waits."

Later that evening, we drove Rachel home. As we entered her driveway, I saw a garage nearby and said there was something about the window. Rachel was astonished when she then realized who I was talking about. Rachel told us that Ed was a middle aged man who had a workshop in the garage. Each morning, he would wait outside the garage and greet her as she left for work. Two years earlier, he shot and killed himself inside the garage and a bullet hit the window. I got out of the car, walked over to the garage, examined the window and saw the bullet hole. Rachel had told Laura the tragic event when it happened but both had forgotten the victim's name until I mentioned it.

GHOST DOG

It was in the news, a few years ago, that the Pope was comforting a young boy whose dog had died. He told the boy that he would see his dog again in Heaven. This brought to mind my own experience about the spirit of a small Sheltie dog that resided in our house for many years and how I helped him pass through the light.

My husband, Al, and I moved into our Natick, Massachusetts house in 1975. After a few months, I started to see, from the corner of my eye, a small brown Sheltie dog walking down the hall. It was usually when I was standing at the bed folding laundry. When I would turn, the dog was gone. This happened every few months and eventually I got used to it.

About eight years ago, we had two small dogs, Duffy and Cindy Lou, who slept in our room. I was usually the last one to go to bed and, each night, I would walk our two dogs down the hall while talking to them and watch them get into their beds that were on the floor. After a few weeks, I noticed another small dog walking alongside us and I felt it rub against my leg. That night, as my husband and I were dozing off, we both heard what sounded like a small dog walking down the hall and stopping at our bedroom door. I immediately got up, turned on the light, opened the door and did not see anything. I checked and saw that Duffy and Cindy Lou were asleep in their beds. I went to the kitchen and opened the basement door and went downstairs and saw our cat, Meowzer, sound asleep in his bed. Each night, the cat would go downstairs and I would close the basement door.

The next night, the same thing happened. We heard the sound of a small dog walking down the hall and stopping at our door but this time we heard what sounded like a dog scratching on the door. Again, I jumped up, turned on the light and opened the door and did not see anything. Our two dogs were asleep in their beds in our room and I, again, went to the basement and saw that Meowzer was sound asleep.

The following night, as I was walking down the hall with our dogs, I was talking to them, as I usually did, and I saw the Sheltie and he was happily walking along with us and was rubbing against me. I felt sorry for him and knew that he should go through the light.

The next day, I spoke to him and told him that I loved him and that he should go through the light where he was supposed to be. Immediately, he left and I never saw him again.

A few weeks later, I was talking with a next door neighbor and she told me about the family who lived in our house about ten years before we moved in. They had a Sheltie puppy that was hit by a car and died in front of our house. He was buried near the pine trees in our back yard.

BRIDGET BISHOP – SALEM WITCH TRIALS

The 'Salem Witch Trials' began in 1692 in Salem, Massachusetts with accusations of witchcraft and ended with the executions of twenty innocent people.

On the morning of Tuesday, June 10, 2015, I posted something on Facebook and, little did I know, that it was the beginning of a chain of spirit communication throughout the day and into the next morning.

In the post, I said that I had just googled a man named Daniel Damon. He lived in the same house in Somerville, Massachusetts that I grew up in except that he lived there in the 1870s. I knew information about him from previous searches and I was hoping to find his picture. It did bring him up but this time, for some reason, it also brought up "The Salem Witch Trials" and a woman named Bridget Bishop who was hung on June 10th in 1692. I do not know why it would bring this woman's information up since she would have nothing to do with the house I grew up in since that house was built in the 1870s. Bridget Bishop was the first person hung for witchcraft during the 'Salem Witch Trials'. Strange still, is that the day of my search, June 10th, was also the same day that she was executed, 323 years earlier.

At that time, the spirit of Bridget Bishop appeared before me and said that she wanted to say something on the anniversary of her hanging. She said to me "He who shineth guilt on the innocent is he himself guilty."

Almost Immediately, I had a vision of my niece Traci and a group of children touring historic places relating to the Witch Trials. Traci lives in Danvers which was part of Salem when the trials occurred. I was just ready to send Traci a Facebook message asking if she had ever taken a tour of the sights but, before I even started typing my message, Traci posted a comment saying that the day before, she and her daughter's third grade class took a tour of historic places relating to the Witch Trials. She thought it strange that I was ready to post what I had just experienced relating to Bridget Bishop when she had just taken a tour relating to this. She was wondering if somehow she had opened a channel for Bridget Bishop to make contact with me.

When Bridget Bishop appeared before me, she was inside what looked like an oval (egg-shaped) clear bubble-like enclosure with a golden light around the perimeter. It was floating in mid-air and she seemed further away from me so she looked smaller but I saw her full body. Her head was mostly down and she was wearing a long brown coat with a hood on her head. She was sad and did not look at me. I wondered if the egg-shaped enclosure could be a time travel vehicle or some sort of energy. It seemed that she was protected by God within the golden perimeter. Usually, the spirits I see look like regular people, in normal size, who come toward me from my right, but there are a few who first appear in front of me. I had never seen a spirit within a bubble.

I asked Renee Richard, a highly respected psychic medium, about the bubble and she said it is very rare and is called a merca-ba which means 'like spirit body' and that part of the spirit travels through dimensions merging lower with higher and that it is the astral part of the person.

As Bridget communicated with me, I asked what I could do to help her and she said to tell the world that she is innocent. She also said that she loved the sound of children's voices singing.

I messaged my niece Traci what Bridget said about the children's voices singing and Traci said that she had a lavender cake mix and that she would make a cake in Bridget's honor. The cake mix actually had little bits of lavender in it. So Traci made a beautiful cake and added vanilla frosting and candles to make it even prettier. Some neighbors just happened to stop by with their children and, along with Traci's 3 little girls, there were five children and they all sang "Happy Birthday" to Bridget" – since that is a song that they were used to singing with a cake, and they had a very happy time. Traci thanked Bridget for the fun celebration and hoped that she liked it.

Right away, Bridget told me to thank Traci and that it brought her great happiness seeing and hearing the children sing. She said it was the happiest time that she can remember. At that moment, she passed through the light and was gone.

The next morning, on Wednesday, June 11th, Traci posted that she was searching on the internet to see where Bridget Bishop's property was in the 1690s and found that today's address would be comparable to 238 Conant Street in Danvers. Coincidently, 238 just happened to be the number of my own street address in Natick, Massachusetts. Another thing that makes this remarkable is that, at the time, Traci's husband worked in an office building that is directly across the street from Bridget's property and he would see it when he looked out his office window. They did not know this until Traci did the search and surprisingly found that Bridget Bishop's house was for sale. Part of the house dates back to the 1690s and was added to over the years. At the same time that her house was for sale, my own house was also for sale.

Another interesting fact is that Bridget Bishop had asked me to tell the world that she is innocent and, at the time of her visit, I was doing international radio shows and I was able to honor her wishes.

CHAPTER 6

UNUSUAL EVENTS

MAPS OF THE BRAIN

On October 7, 1992, I was in Rochester, New York with my husband, Al, and our three children, attending my mother-in-law's funeral. My sister-in-law, Iris, had a gathering of family and friends to her home after the funeral. This was the first time that I had met her friends. I walked into the kitchen and five of her friends were standing around talking. They had heard that I was psychic and proceeded to ask me to tell them about themselves. I went to the first person and said that I envisioned a ring with a blue stone that she was receiving as a gift and I told her about her daughter's ballet recital and some other non-earth shattering things. She said that her boyfriend was giving her a ring with a blue stone that she had picked it out the day before and she was waiting for it to be resized. She also said that her twelve year old daughter was getting ready for her ballet recital.

I went to the next person and told him some things about where he works and the names of his associates. I then went to the next person and told her a few accurate but uninteresting things.

The fourth person was a professional looking man with a beard and I sensed that he did not believe in psychics and was blocking me. I continued to the next person and told her some things about her family and the recent vacation they were on. I went around again and looked at each person and I was still blocked by the man with the beard. I went around for a third time, stopping at each person, but not saying anything. When I arrived at the man, everything opened up and I could read him. I described in detail the exterior of the building he worked in, including the street address. I said that I did not know what he did for a living but that I saw maps in blue and brown that looked like geography maps. I saw the maps as though I were floating high above them. I mentioned a man named Eugene in California. I then envisioned the bearded man doing something astonishing, and I said to the group that I was hesitant to tell them what I saw. They all asked me to continue, including the man himself and his wife who was standing next to him. I told them that I saw the man putting a sharp object into the top of a head. The man stood there with a shocked look on his face. He told me that he is a neurologist and he does experiments on monkeys' brains using sharp objects. He said that the maps, that I saw, were maps of the brain that were in blue and brown. He said he received the maps from a colleague named Eugene who lives in California. It was all very interesting, especially for a neurologist who did not believe in psychic abilities until the gathering in the kitchen.

SYRACUSE UNIVERSITY – BOOK OF NAMES

My niece, Ardis, lives in Rochester, New York. A number of years ago, when she was a student at Syracuse University, she would occasionally telephone her Uncle Al and me to say hello and ask me to use my psychic abilities. During one of our phone conversations, I told her that I saw an old red book in the main room of her dormitory building that has the names of hundreds of people, handwritten in over the years. I told her what page number to look at and that she would find a particular name on that page. Amazingly, each page that I told her to look at, she did find the name I mentioned. This was a great source of entertainment and bewilderment. I can understand if she was already looking at a particular name on a certain page, then I would suggest that I was using telepathy by reading her mind; but that was not the case, especially since the book was closed when I told her what pages to look at to find particular names. I felt I was there in the dormitory building, looking at the book myself and seeing the names on certain pages. I do not understand why I was able to do this since I was almost three hundred miles away and had never been to Syracuse University and had no previous knowledge of the dormitory building or the book.

I also told Ardis that, many years before, there was a young lady who hung herself in the dormitory building because she was accused of something that she did not do. Ardis said that there was a rumor of a girl who worked there years before. She was falsely accused of stealing jewelry and hung herself. She was later proven to be innocent.

During another phone conversation, I told Ardis that I saw 'Kensington Gardens', the name 'Muldoon' and the word 'maroon'. She then told me she was going to Kensington Gardens and planned to spend a semester in England but she did not know what the 'Muldoon' and 'maroon' meant. She found the answers on her plane flight to England. The flight attendants wore 'maroon' outfits and one of them was wearing a name tag that said 'Anne Muldoon'.

One day, Ardis and three of her college friends came to my house to visit. They were anxious to see what I would predict for their futures. I told one of them that her future husband was a big teddy bear kind of guy with a nice personality, that he wore plaid shirts, jeans and boots and owned a dog and a blue pick-up truck. She met and married the man I described about three years later. I told one of the other girls that she would meet her future husband when she was eating a piece of cake. Two years later, she was at the wedding reception of a friend. She was eating a piece of cake when a nice young man came over to her table and was introduced. She married him the next year. I told the third girl that her boyfriend had some connection with a diamond. She said he was stationed at Diamond Head Island with the military. I told Ardis that her future husband was standing in front of a wall of books and that she would have to wait until she was at least thirty to marry him. She met her attorney (now a judge) husband a decade later.

Ardis's brother, Jason, called me around the same time to ask if he would be going to his high school prom. I told him that he would bring a girl that has a name similar to 'Finnegan' and that she would ask Jason's opinion about what dress she should wear – the pink one or the black one. About a month later, Jason asked a pretty classmate to accompany him to the prom. She asked him which dress he preferred – the pink one or the black one. He told her the pink one and that is the one she wore. Her last name was 'Finnimen'.

THE BANK VAULT

In 2000, I was working as the administrative manager for a company in Wellesley Hills, Massachusetts. We were located on the first floor of an attractive professional building on the corner of the street. Our part of the building was once a bank and the round deposit drop off door was still in place on the front of the building. The bank vault was at the back of the office and was used to store file cabinets filled with closed sales folders. The vault's heavy door was propped wide open with a large rock. Heaven forbid if anyone were searching for an old file, alone, late at night and the door should shut.

The first day that I entered the office and walked down the narrow hall to the vault area, I sensed a man in his early fifties standing near the vault door. He was dressed in a vintage 1930s dark brown three piece suit and wore brown shoes. He looked worried and kept looking at the pocket watch that he held in his hand. The watch had a gold chain that connected to his vest pocket. His dark hair was glossy and straight and slicked back firmly against his head. He was clean shaven and attractive, and if he was not dead, I would say he looked to be in the prime of life. The market had gone down drastically and everything he had in the bank was gone. He waited at the vault door peering into the vault and his eyes never focused on mine, he was in his own world. I sensed his name was George.

I never told anyone about George until he was sighted months later by another employee. The receptionist's desk was at the front of the office. One day, she came running into my office, visibly shaken. She said she had just seen a ghost. She had been sitting at her desk and noticed, from the corner of her eye, a person walking toward her. She looked up and saw a man walk by her desk and go through a solid partition toward the deposit drop off door. She said he was dressed in an old fashioned brown suit and had dark hair combed back. There was no way the man could have come from the area where she first noticed him because the door to enter the office was straight in front of her and he did not come through the door. I told her that perhaps she saw someone walking down the street in front of our building but she insisted the man was in the office and walked right in front of her desk and straight through the partition. I mentioned this to Denise, one of our associates, and we kept it to ourselves.

About three months later, a new employee, Maudie, joined our office. One day, she heard Denise and me mention a ghost. Maudie stopped dead in her tracks as she walked past my office. She said "Ghost, what ghost? Why didn't anyone tell me about a ghost?" Maudie then related a terrifying experience she had the first month of working there. She had stopped by one night to use the fax machine. She came in through the front door and turned on some of the lights. The fax machine was located on the inside of the front counter. She had just finished faxing and was getting ready to leave when she saw a man walking straight toward her. She was very frightened as she thought that she was alone. The man walked up to the outside of the counter, looked straight through her, then turned and walked toward the narrow hall where the vault was and disappeared.

Maudie grabbed her purse and ran out the front door, not thinking if she left the lights on or the door unlocked. She never told anyone because she thought she would be laughed at. I asked Maudie what the man looked like. She said he was dressed in an old fashioned three-piece suit and his hair was dark and combed back. That particular office is no longer in existence but George is probably still standing at the vault door.

CHURCH OF SPIRITS

This is one of the strangest cases that I have ever been asked to help with. The setting is a Catholic Church property that includes three separate buildings – the church, the rectory and the school. The property was sold by the Boston Archdiocese to a developer who turned the buildings into well-appointed condominiums. The renovations kept intact the elegance of the original high ceilings, large windows and doors, mahogany woodwork and staircases.

I arrived home from work one evening, in October 2009, and noticed my kitchen phone light blinking, signaling that someone had left a message. It was a cryptic message from Linda, a real estate agent, who said she needed my help and to call her as soon as possible. I tossed my coat and purse on the kitchen table and dialed her number. She answered right away and was speaking so quickly that she did not seem to be able to catch her breath. The bits and pieces of what she was saying came together like a jig saw puzzle and I could see the dilemma that had been unfolding for many months. She said she recently called the Boston Archdiocese, asking for their help, and was put through to an answering machine where she did leave a message but no one called her back.

I asked her if she had mentioned in the message what the problem was and she said she did not. She really needed to speak to a person not an answering machine.

Linda related that Nancy, the first owner of one of the condominiums to move in, was experiencing unusual activity in the rectory building where she lives. Nancy said she heard walking in the reception hall, many times at night, and that it happened between eight o'clock in the evening and four o'clock in the morning. One night, about three months earlier, she was in bed, just dozing off, when she heard walking and then the sound of an old fashioned buzzer. She woke up and heard a woman's voice say "Do you know that it's ten o'clock in the evening?" Nancy wondered who could be speaking through the intercom. She got out of bed, put on her robe and opened the door to her second floor condo. This led to the reception area. She walked down the stairs, went to the front glass double doors and looked outside. There was no one there so she turned around to go back upstairs. When she turned around, she was startled by the appearance of a woman with long dark hair, wearing an old fashioned dress, standing at the bottom of the stairs. The apparition disappeared and Nancy rushed upstairs, ran inside her condo, and shut and locked the door.

Three weeks later, in the early hours of Sunday morning, Nancy was again awakened by the sound of an old fashioned buzzer. This time, the woman's voice said "What are you doing at two thirty in the morning?" The next day, Nancy was having a dinner party and was sitting in the living room with some of her guests. While she was talking about what had happened early that morning, she and one of the guests saw a woman, dressed in a nun's habit, walk through a closed closet door into the kitchen then disappear. Later that week, Linda was told of an earlier incident that happened in the church building. A workman was alone in the steeple standing on a ladder. A piece of molding fell from the ceiling and he went down the ladder to pick it up. After picking up the molding, he stood up to go back up the ladder and there was a bearded man with a golden aura standing in front of him. The workman was so frightened that he dropped the molding and ran out of the church. He told the developer what he had seen and the developer did not believe him. The workman is a quiet young man who would be one of the last people you would suspect to make up such a story.

Linda asked me if I would meet her and the condo owner, Nancy, at the property, some evening at ten o'clock since the sound of walking happens at night. The following Sunday, my husband, Al, and I drove to the church, parked in the rectory parking lot and waited for Linda and her husband to arrive. About ten minutes later, we saw the headlights of an approaching car and I called Linda from my cell phone to confirm it was her. The weather was unusual for October with large snowflakes falling most of the day and melting as they hit the ground. The four of us got out of our cars, went to the rectory building and Nancy buzzed us inside. As we entered the building, past the double glass doors, I felt that I had walked back in time. Hanging on the walls of the lobby were black and white photos of long dead priests, nuns and students. There was a silence and stillness in the air and I felt that we were being watched. We walked up the stairs to the second floor, walked down the corridor to Nancy's door and knocked gently. Nancy was anxiously awaiting our arrival and welcomed us inside. The new and upscale were contained within the walls of long ago.

I brought a steno pad to take notes and a tape recorder. As we followed Nancy through the rooms, she told us what she had been experiencing for many months and it was determined that the paranormal activity began when renovations on the church building itself started. Nancy told us that recently the footsteps were heard inside her condo at night. She would be in bed and hear someone walking down the hall outside her bedroom and the sound would always stop at her bedroom door that she kept locked at night. Her cat, Napoleon, slept on Nancy's bed and he would sit up and be alert to the sounds of the footsteps and look at something that could not be seen.

Nancy has psychic abilities and was not frightened by what was going on but she felt uneasy. I went to the closet door that the nun was seen walking through and I envisioned what it looked like many years before. I asked if it was a hall before it was a closet. Linda told me that originally it was a hall that you walked through to go to a bathroom. That bathroom area is now part of the kitchen. I opened the closet door and looked inside. There was a large temperature control unit that filled up most of the space. The unit was off. I closed the closet door, placed my hand on it and concentrated. The rest of the group was quietly standing nearby watching me. After a few moments, the room became ice cold. It was so cold that you could see your breath. I spoke to the spirits who were earthbound and told them they should go to the light and pass through. I felt two female souls pass over and the coldness went away and the room's temperature was back to normal. One of the souls passed over quickly but the other was hesitant and felt she had to stay. I told her that her loved ones were waiting for her on the other side and I guided her over. I felt her emotions to hold on to her past. I told her that the building was no longer part of a church and explained what condominiums are, that they are similar to apartments and that people buy them. I felt that the first spirit who had passed over was now waiting to help this reluctant spirit through the light. Finally they were both on the other side and everything was calm again.

Linda started telling Nancy about the bearded man with the golden aura that the workman saw in the steeple. Nancy had not heard about it and related something unusual she had seen on a few occasions early in the morning. She gets up around five o'clock each morning, makes her coffee and brings a cup to the living room window and looks out onto the quiet darkened street. Her living room faces the steeple and she has seen a glowing figure of a man walking inside the church, past the windows on the floor directly below the steeple. We found out that other neighbors have also seen the glowing man early in the morning walking past the church windows.

Things were quiet for many months after my visit. No more reports of walking, no more buzzers, no more voices. Even the cat, Napoleon, slept in comfort and was not awakened by something you could not see but then the activity started up again.

One day, Nancy had a friend over and she had not told him about the unusual occurrences. As he was walking into the living room, he noticed a woman sitting in a chair with a priest standing behind her. They disappeared after a few seconds. More stories started to filter in about other occupants having paranormal activity. One such person is a no-nonsense man who has been experiencing such things since he moved in about a month after Nancy. He finally felt comfortable enough to talk about it. He has two bedrooms in his condo that are across the hall from each other. Many nights, while he is in his bedroom, he hears a woman and man having a conversation in the bedroom across the hall. He said this has been going on for quite some time but it does not bother him.

Around the same time, one of the developers and two of his workmen were having lunch while sitting at a round table in the church building. A woman, wearing a long dress, appeared out of nowhere, walked around the table and disappeared into thin air.

Many long-time neighbors have said that the church property has been known to be haunted for years. There are earthbound souls there and they are reluctant to leave because they feel a connection to the property. It was a comforting place for many and perhaps not for others. It was their church, their school, a place for family gatherings, for special occasions – a connection that is difficult to take from them. They need to be comforted on this side so they can be guided to pass over and find peace. There are many places like this all over the world and some have fallen to ruin and others, like this church property, have found a new life.

POTTING SOIL

A few years ago, my friend, Pat, invited a group of ladies to a jewelry party at her house in Littleton, Massachusetts. As I walked inside the kitchen, Pat introduced me to Jill and told her that I was a psychic. Jill, who fashions beautiful jewelry using high quality crystal beads and silver, was sitting at the kitchen table surrounded by small gift boxes filled with bracelets, necklaces, earrings and other creations. She asked me to use my psychic abilities to find her friend's car keys. I immediately envisioned a two car garage with two cars inside. I told Jill that the brown car on the left was the one that her friend drove. I walked into the garage and on the left side, against the wall, I saw something that looked like small shelves. I said that the keys were sometimes put on a shelf and they had fallen. Under the shelves, I saw a large mound of dark greasy looking dirt on the floor and said that if her friend looks on the floor, to be careful because his hands will get very dirty sifting through the dirt. I told her that there was a container with a red label nearby. Jill had never been to the friend's house so she did not know what his garage looked like and what was inside.

The next day, Jill called me and said she had just spoken to her friend and gave him the information that I came up with. His car keys had been missing for a few weeks and another set had been ordered so it was not an emergency that he should find the missing set. He confirmed that he does have a two car garage, has a brown car and parks it on the left side inside the garage. On the left wall, at the back, is a ladder and he often put his car keys on one of the rungs. Under the ladder, on the floor, was a large pile of dark shiny dirt that had fallen out of a large broken bag of potting soil. Jill's friend said that when his keys went missing, he sifted through the dirt but his hands got so dirty that he decided to stop. He had not found the keys elsewhere so there was a very good chance they could have been right there under the ladder, next to the container with the red label.

MISSING GIRL FOUND

On Tuesday morning, February 23rd, 2010, something told me to get to work early so that I could stop into the insurance office next to mine. I walked in, introduced myself to the two ladies who work there and told them that I was a psychic and I sensed that someone in the office needed my help. We did not know each other very well and I was not even sure of their names. They were both very interested in what I was saying and one of them started to cry. She asked if I could find her boyfriend's daughter who he has been trying to find for over nine years. I told her that I would help find the daughter and I sent good positive energy to encircle the girl and bring her home. I felt she was in danger and needed guidance.

The next morning, when I arrived at work, I opened my computer and saw that the lady in the next office had left a comment on my blog. I went next door and as I walked in, she said she was just talking about me and was telling her co-worker what happened the night before. The missing girl called her father the previous evening and was coming home. The two ladies and I were very emotional, hugging and crying with joy. The next day, the father met his daughter and brought her home and everyone is doing very well.

The following is the message that I received when I arrived at my office that morning: "Donna, we spoke the other day before work in our office. I told you I had just traveled out of state to try to find my boyfriend's daughter that he has not seen for over nine years. She just called tonight. It is a miracle. I know I had asked you for help."

SWEDISH FISH

Many people have unusual things happen to them every so often. This particular occurrence is certainly on my list. In 2001, I was on my lunch break with Susan, a co-worker. We had gone for a walk and stopped inside a bakery on our way back to the office. We had never visited the bakery before and Susan wanted to look at the cakes for her mother's birthday. Amongst the display of appetizing pastries were frosted cupcakes with Swedish Fish candies on top. We talked about the Swedish Fish as we left the bakery and walked along the sidewalk. A car pulled up to the curb and stopped. It was my husband, Al, on his way to work. Susan and I went over to the car as Al lowered the passenger side window. He greeted us with a smile, extended his arm and opened his hand. In his hand, he held Swedish Fish candies that he had taken out of the bag he had just purchased at a convenience store a few miles away. He handed Susan and me the bag and offered us some. It was a rare occasion when Al or I bought Swedish Fish which made this event something to think about.

CHAPTER 8

CONTACT WITH AL

My beloved husband, Al, passed away on March 17, 2012. When we learned that he had about a year to live, he told me that when he passed, he would try to communicate with me to prove there is an afterlife – and he has.

One of those times was a few weeks after he passed. I had gone out to the driveway to pick up the morning newspaper and was sitting up in bed reading it. All of a sudden, there was the usual, somewhat loud, sound that Al made while putting my coffee cup down on my night stand. He would always, jokingly, make it loud to get my attention. I turned around and there he was, standing only inches away, smiling at me and looking great. He then turned, walked into the hall and disappeared. I jumped up and followed him but he was gone.

A few weeks later, I was, again, sitting up in bed reading the morning newspaper when I heard three very loud knocks on my night stand. You would need to hit the wooden night stand very hard to get the same loud sound. I got up and looked all around the night stand and knocked on it myself. It took a lot of strength to get the same sound with my knuckles. Then six days later, I, again, was reading the morning newspaper and there were two very loud knocks on Al's night stand. I jumped up and said to him that I know it is him and that I know what his message is. He would often write me little notes that said "I love you Donna." Though it took six days for the entire message to come through, I realized what it said. The first three knocks on my night stand said "I love you" and the two knocks on his night stand said "Donna".

Then there is the energy that he sends to my right hand, as though he is holding it. About a month after he passed, my daughter, Alicia, was visiting me when the living room filled with a great energy and I could feel Al holding my right hand. Alicia then held my hand and she felt the strong energy that stayed with her for a day.

Another time, I had my friend, Patty, over at lunch and we were sitting in the living room. She asked me to play the piano and as I was playing, I looked over and Patty was crying. She said that while I was playing the piano, the living room filled up with a beautiful loving energy and a whitish grey mist appeared around me and it formed into Al.

A similar thing happened, a few weeks later, when I was ready to play the piano at the hospital where I volunteered. It is the same hospital where Al passed way. I was speaking with an acquaintance and she called me the next day to tell me of the unusual occurrence that happened the day before. She said that, while we were talking the day before, a whitish grey mist formed beside me and turned into Al. She could not say anything at the time because there were people in the lobby but she wanted me to know.

Al appeared to me for a few months after he passed away. Since then, I continue to feel his energy and, at times, his presence.

I have spoken with others who have lost loved ones and some have had similar experiences where they have seen and communicated with their loved ones.

CHAPTER 9

A GLIMPSE OF HEAVEN
MY NEAR DEATH EXPERIENCE

I stood at my front door watching the morning rush hour traffic drive by and anxiously waited for the ambulance to arrive. I had called 911 a short time before and stayed on the phone with the nice lady who answered. She took my information and reassured me that the ambulance was on its way. I asked her name and she said "Donna", a name I will always remember since it is the same name as mine. A short time later, I saw the ambulance driving up the street and I told Donna that the ambulance was arriving and I was hanging up the phone. I put the phone back inside the kitchen and got my cell phone from my purse. I called my daughter, Alicia, and told her that I was not feeling well and had called an ambulance. The thought crossed my mind that it could be the last time I would speak with her.

It was Valentine's Day 2014 but it did not mean much to me since I had lost my husband, Al, to cancer two years before. I suppose if one were to have a heart problem it may as well be on Valentine's Day. The thought of writing my own obituary with the wording "She died of a broken heart." was too dramatic and, somehow, I knew that I would be okay but there was always the possibility.

At the same time that Al was diagnosed with cancer, I got Atrial Fibrillation which is an electrical problem with the heart. The doctors said that mine was caused by stress which is a common factor when a loved one is very ill. They tried medications but they did not seem to help, so that morning, I woke up around five o'clock with my heart beating very fast. I sat up in bed, thinking my heart rate would go back to normal but it did not. I then thought that I had better get ready to go to the hospital, not realizing how very serious it was and that I should hurry. Instead, I took a shower, washed my hair, made the bed, packed a bag and wasted time. When you have always been healthy, it is hard to believe that death can be so close and every second counts. I knocked on my son Jonathan's door to ask if he was going to work since he would always leave by seven thirty and it was now an hour later. He said he did not have to be at work until eleven because of the snow storm that we had the previous night. I then told him that I did not feel well and that I was calling 911. He said he would bring me to the hospital but something told me not to wait any longer and I dialed 911.

Jonathan's car was parked in the driveway and he followed me outside. As I walked towards the ambulance, an EMT asked if I was going to move the car and I told him that I was the patient. He said in bewilderment "You're the patient! – don't walk; we will come to get you." Something told me to keep walking and not to wait for the stretcher to be taken out of the back of the ambulance and carried to my house. Then I would have been put on the stretcher and carried back to the ambulance. I felt a little better being outside in the cool air and a neighbor ran over to see if there was anything she could do. I looked at the high step I would have to take to get inside of the ambulance and realized I did not have the energy to try. The EMTs got the stretcher from the ambulance, put me on it, lifted me inside and shut the door while Jonathan waited outside. Once inside the ambulance, one of the EMTs told the others that my heart rate was very high. I asked him "How high?" and he did not tell me. I heard him say to the others "70 over 50" and I knew that was my blood pressure going down and I was in danger. Within seconds, I started to slip away and I heard myself calmly say to the EMTs "I'm going, I'm going, I'm going." I then heard an EMT say

"Get the paddles!" I felt my spirit rising up and saw my body lying on the stretcher. I sat up then stood up and started walking and going upward. As I walked along, I saw the inside of the ambulance in great detail and everything was illuminated by a white light. I saw an EMT reaching for something that was hanging on the inside of the ambulance. Everything earthly seemed trivial and it did not bother me that I was leaving. I felt I was going home. I was lifted up to a higher plain and walked along a serene path where everything was pure, white and spiritual. It was the most beautiful feeling imaginable. I came to a threshold and stopped. I could not go any further because my left foot was up to the entrance and I would have had to take one more step with my right foot to enter.

I looked down at my feet and saw a white line that divides Heaven and Earth. I could see past the entrance and there was a long white walkway with white walls and a white ceiling. Everything was silent and I sensed that if I walked over the line, I would be bathed in a golden light and be with my loved ones who had passed. Within seconds, they appeared – my husband, my parents and there were others that I did not yet recognize since they were further away but getting closer. I then heard a kind and loving fatherly voice say that it was my decision to take the step to pass over but that it was not my time and that I had many more years and things to do on Earth. I was also told that time is different there and that the many years ahead would seem like seconds to them. I thought of my three children and how they would be devastated to lose their mother since they had lost their father two years before and I thought of the three EMTs who were trying to save my life and how they would feel if I passed. I did not feel anything when the defibrillator was used to restart my heart. I was awake and felt fine. I never thought of the meaning of the phrase 'on the line' until my 'Near Death Experience'. The next day, while at the hospital, Jonathan said that one of the EMTs told him I had been 'on the line'. I had not yet mentioned my experience to Jonathan before this.

It felt that there were others around me that day guiding me and making sure that I made the right decisions. Even the doctor at the nearest hospital, where I was taken, said it was my decision to go to any hospital I wanted. I opted to be taken to Massachusetts General in Boston since that is where my surgeon was, and after staying at the nearest hospital for about five hours, I was brought to Mass General by ambulance. On that ride to Boston, an EMT stayed with me in the back of the ambulance. We had a nice talk and I told him about my 'Near Death Experience'. He said that he had heard similar stories from others.

A few months later, on May 23rd, I had a catheter heart ablation at Massachusetts General Hospital that corrected the electrical issue. I am very fortunate to be healthy with no heart or medical problems. Three years before, also on May 23rd, my husband had his surgery at Massachusetts General Hospital. Mine was originally scheduled for June 10th but, due to my being rushed to the hospital, I had my procedure on the same date at the same hospital but three years apart. When I told a nurse, she asked if I wanted to change the date of my surgery and I told her I did not.

I am blessed to have glimpsed a little piece of Heaven. It proved to me that all of the wonderful things that we have heard about the afterlife are true.

CHAPTER 10

MEETING BETTY HILL - UFO CASE 'THE INTERRUPTED JOURNEY'

I can never forget the night that my sister, Bess, frantically, but quietly, said "Get down! We're being invaded!", as I entered the living room on my way to my bedroom. I thought she was kidding until I saw it too. It was the 1960s and, at the time, I was a young teen and she was a no-nonsense fourth grade school teacher. We had just watched our usual Sunday evening television shows 'What's My Line' and 'I've Got a Secret' and she had gone into the living room before me. It was her habit, each night, to look out the front living room window to be sure her car was okay. This particular night was much different than any other. She had just looked outside and almost screamed and quickly crouched down on one side of the window. As I entered the living room, she told me to get down and to watch from the opposite side of the window. I could not believe what was happening.

The house across the street was where our eldest sister, Elsie, lived with her husband and their three children. About thirty feet above the roof of their house was a large round reddish orange luminous object. It was bigger than a harvest moon and looked similar to a piece of scenery hanging in the sky. Being of logical mind, I tried to figure out what the object could be. I thought that since Harvard University and MIT were nearby, could it possibly be a halogram or similar, a science project perhaps? But that explanation did not make sense when it acted as an actual object and took off at a tremendous speed and disappeared over the horizon. We were fortunate to live on the top floor of a house with unobstructed views and Bess and I kept our eyes on the object until it was out of sight. We did not talk about it much except with a few family members and then we put it in the past and rarely mentioned it. Eventually, I found out that there were similar encounters in the 1960s, not just in New England but in other parts of the world. One of the most famous UFO cases is that of Betty and Barney Hill who encountered a round reddish orange luminous object as they drove home, one night, through the White Mountains of New Hampshire on their way from a vacation in Canada. The object landed and turned into a round metallic disk. According to the Hills, they were captured and brought aboard the object where the occupants did medical procedures on them. Theirs is one of two landmark cases that are in one book 'Incident at Exeter' 'The Interrupted Journey'.

Coincidently, about ten years after Bess's and my encounter, I was working at the New England Conservatory of Music and was asked by a co-worker, Johanna, if I would like to meet Betty Hill who was giving a talk at a church in New Hampshire. I asked her if I could ask my friend Terri to join us and she said she could. Johanna drove us to the church and there was Betty, dressed in a pants suit, greeting people. She gave a descriptive recollection of hers and Barney's encounter and, afterwards, she sat on the floor and answered questions. I found it very interesting that her description of the UFO, that she and Barney saw, was the same as what my sister and I saw, pertaining to the round reddish orange luminous object. I am thankful that it did not turn into a metallic disk when I saw it as that would have been quite overwhelming.

It would be interesting to learn of other people's UFO encounters. Perhaps some of the readers would like to share their own experiences with me.

DONNA DIPIETRO is a psychic medium and paranormal investigator. In 2008, she was invited to Boston's famed Isabella Stewart Gardner Museum to help solve the biggest art heist in history. Her great accuracy provided valuable information that led to the identities of two of the robbery suspects and where they were from. Donna has the gift of precognition and predicted that Pope John Paul II would be shot twenty-four hours before it happened. She has spoken and written in languages, that she does not understand, to get messages across to loved ones from the other side. She has found missing children and missing valuables, has helped on murder investigations and visited many haunted places to guide spirits to the light. She had an amazing Near Death Experience and has had contact with her beloved husband, Al, who passed away in 2012. Donna is a professional pianist, published short story writer, radio talk show host and a guest speaker, including at 'Mystery Writers of America'.

CONCLUSION

I would like to use my gift, in a larger extent, to help others, and I believe one way is with the help of radio and TV shows, international conferences and psychic associations. In that case, we can unite people in the psychic community to use good positive energy to make the world a better place for everyone.

Made in the USA
Middletown, DE
05 December 2020